SCHOOL REFORM

A SPECIAL REPORT

School Reform

LESSONS FROM ENGLAND

KATHRYN STEARNS

WITH A FOREWORD BY
ERNEST L. BOYER

THE CARNEGIE FOUNDATION
FOR THE ADVANCEMENT OF TEACHING

5 IVY LANE, PRINCETON, NEW JERSEY 08540

Copyright © 1996

The Carnegie Foundation
for the Advancement of Teaching

All rights reserved. No part of this book may be reproduced in any form—except for brief quotations not to exceed one thousand words in a review or professional work—without permission in writing from the publisher.

This report is published as part of the effort by The Carnegie Foundation for the Advancement of Teaching to explore significant issues in education. The views expressed should not necessarily be ascribed to individual members of the Board of Trustees of The Carnegie Foundation.

LIBRARY OF CONGRESS CATALOGING-IN-PUBLICATION DATA

Stearns, Kathryn, date.
   School reform : lessons from England / Kathryn Stearns ; with a foreword by Ernest L. Boyer.
       p.   cm. — (A special report)
   Includes bibliographical references (p.   ) and index.
   ISBN 0-931050-57-X
   1. School management and organization—England. 2. Educational change—England. 3. Curriculum change—England. 4. Education and state—England. 5. School management and organization—United States.
I. Title. II. Series : Special report (Carnegie Foundation for the Advancement of Teaching)
LB2901.S74 1996
371.2'00942—dc20   96-1687

Copies are available from

CALIFORNIA PRINCETON FULFILLMENT SERVICES
1445 Lower Ferry Road
Ewing, New Jersey 08618

TOLL-FREE—U.S. & CANADA (800) 777-4726   FAX (800) 999-1958

PHONE (609) 833-1759   FAX (609) 883-7413

THIS CARNEGIE FOUNDATION REPORT was developed and written during the presidential tenure of Dr. Ernest L. Boyer, who died on December 8, 1995. It is published in grateful memory of his vision, his leadership, and his service.

CONTENTS

ACKNOWLEDGMENTS		ix
FOREWORD	*by Ernest L. Boyer*	xi
INTRODUCTION	*Snapshots from Abroad*	3
CHAPTER I	*Standards: Going for Control*	9
CHAPTER II	*Autonomy: Going It Alone*	33
CHAPTER III	*Choice: Going to Market*	69
CHAPTER IV	*The Picture of Reform*	87
APPENDIX	*Site Visits*	95
NOTES		99
INDEX		109

ACKNOWLEDGMENTS

First and foremost, I want to express my gratitude to Ernest L. Boyer. Without Dr. Boyer's interest and support, my observations from England would not have become a special report for The Carnegie Foundation. I am tremendously grateful for the enthusiasm he brought to the project, for his professional advice, and for his respect and friendship during the all-too-brief time of our collaboration. I deeply regret that Dr. Boyer did not see the printed book.

The first-hand testimony of teachers, parents, administrators, and many others was essential to this report. I am indebted to all those who conducted tours of their schools and explained how the legislated changes have affected them. I'd like to thank particularly headteachers Brigid Beattie, K. H. Brooke, Bernard Clark, Peter Downes, Michael Duffy, Peter Jenkins, Peter Hore, Mike Read, Martin Roberts, Anne Rumney, and Stephen Szemerenyi.

Chief education officers in the boroughs, cities, and counties also helped to put the reforms into perspective. My appreciation to Keith Anderson in Gloucestershire, Tim Brighouse in Birmingham, Peter Mitchell in Camden, Donald Naismith in Wandsworth, Roy Pryke in Kent, and Christopher Tipple in Northumberland.

Representatives of the largest teachers' unions made helpful suggestions for site visits. Clive Andrews opened doors at the city technology colleges.

I am also grateful to all those who shared their research findings. At the University of London, Caroline Gipps (Institute of Education) and Paul Black (King's College) provided essential technical background on assessment; John Tomlinson and his colleagues at Warwick University answered questions about the curriculum and grant-maintained schools;

Ron Glatter and Philip Woods at the Open University shared their data on the effects of school choice, as did Stephen Ball of King's College.

A heartfelt thanks to the editor-in-chief of the *Times Educational Supplement*, Patricia Rowan, who introduced me to the issues and to many of the insiders. Her help, from beginning to end, was invaluable.

Robert Hochstein, assistant to the president and director of communications for The Carnegie Foundation, has been an ally throughout. I thank him for serving as my trans-Atlantic link and for critiquing drafts.

I am grateful to George Adams, my husband Robert Bruce, and others at the law offices of Debevoise and Plimpton in London, where I frequently trespassed. The firm's photocopiers and other technological aids helped speed the manuscript to Princeton.

Stuart Maclure's history of the 1988 Education Reform Act, *Education Re-formed*, served as a basic reference book. The few footnotes that appear belie my frequent reliance on his guide to the law.

Jan Hempel, editor at the Foundation, saw the manuscript through editing and production with great patience.

Thanks, finally, to my two young children, Hannah and David, who tried very hard to obey the sign they posted one day on my door: "Ofis. Plese nock." We're working on spelling reforms.

KATHRYN STEARNS

London
January 1996

FOREWORD

by Ernest L. Boyer

EDUCATION REFORM knows no boundaries. Throughout the world, countries strive to improve their schools, boost student achievement, and help prepare graduates for productive lives. In both East and West, in countries as different and as far apart as New Zealand and the Netherlands, reformers are seeking to raise curriculum standards, rebuild governance structures, and expand options for selecting schools.

In this new study, we turn to England, where many trends in education reform converge. In the past decade, the British government imposed a national curriculum, embraced open enrollment and, most consequentially perhaps, shifted decision-making authority away from the district offices to the schools themselves. Most of these reforms, contained in a single Act of Parliament enacted in 1988, were intended to make schools more effective, more efficient, and more responsive to the discipline of competition. They challenged long-held assumptions and established practices, from the role of administrators, teachers, and parents, to the purpose of schooling itself.

British educators and policymakers have, in recent years, grappled with some tough questions. Are classroom standards sufficiently high? Should the curriculum be entrusted to teachers alone? Do district control and local bureaucracy prevent flexibility and stifle innovation at the school level? What are parents' rights in determining where their children should attend school? For anyone following the path of reform in the United States, the questions are familiar—and timely.

When Kathryn Stearns, an experienced journalist on leave from the *Washington Post*'s editorial page, offered to dispatch to us her observations of school reform in England, we eagerly accepted. A perspective from abroad could, we believe, help inform our debate here, because the issues, if not the answers, are so congruent. As a senior fellow for the Foundation, Stearns spent many months touring the country, visiting schools, auditing classroom lessons, talking to headteachers (principals) and regional education officers, interviewing civil servants and academicians, and sifting through research pertaining to the national curriculum, assessment, local management, self-governing schools, and school choice.

This report focuses on three key topics of overlapping interest and concern: *standards, school autonomy,* and *school choice.* Our purpose is not to pass judgment. What is right for one country is, of course, not necessarily right for another. But we think it's useful to learn more about policies and practices in England that bear striking parallels to reforms—both legislated and proposed—in districts and states across America. Our hope is that this study of English school reform will broaden our perspective and increase our understanding of America's own efforts to improve schools.

While states and some professional associations here have been working to develop curriculum standards and frameworks, legislation in England gave the national government the authority to mandate the "knowledge, skills and understanding" expected of all students. A hasty first attempt at a national curriculum was rejected by most teachers and parents for being too complex and prescriptive. The government has since revised the standards, this time in consultation with teachers and administrators. The resultant curriculum has been more warmly received and illustrates how voluntary standards, carefully crafted, might be used in this country to examine course content and assess what takes place in the classroom.

The English perspective on school choice is likewise instructive. The government's reforms closely linked accountability with a more competitive market in British education. A variety of incentives, from self-governing schools to open enrollment, were enacted to open up the marketplace and give parents greater influence over education. In reality, however, families who seek a school outside their own neighborhood can face many constraints; in the most competitive areas, for example, schools are more likely to choose students than vice versa, resulting in confusion, frustration, and disappointment. Here again, there are striking parallels with the American experience, and lessons to be learned.

Curriculum reform and school choice in England are interesting and relevant to reforms here, but we were especially impressed by England's recent experience as it relates to school governance—to the matter of how local schools are controlled.

Here in America education was, for more than three centuries, primarily a local affair. In 1647, the Massachusetts Bay Colony decreed that all towns and villages of fifty or more citizens should hire a schoolmaster to teach the children to read and write. This declaration not only affirmed the importance of literacy, it also established education as a responsibility of each community. Our deeply held belief in local school control, as a grass-roots effort, has long dominated the nation's attitudes about the governance of education.

A century or so ago, however, state education departments began to assert themselves, and more recently, through programs for the disadvantaged, for example, the federal government has established a stronger partnership in education. Still, thoughtful, large-scale planning about how we should run our schools has been for the most part absent, and what's emerged is a "nonsystem system," one with an almost hopelessly confusing pattern of rules and regulations and overlapping jurisdictions. While the federal government talks about national goals and standards, the states have been exercising more and more control. In addition, more than sixteen thousand school districts have become more aggressively involved in the oversight of classroom education.

Many of these district offices, especially those in our besieged urban centers, have larger staffs than some state education departments. They have assumed a behemoth-like quality, making administration an end in itself. Schools are left immobilized, unable to make key decisions about their budgets, their buildings, and their programs—an irony, because district superintendencies were intended originally to bestow order on the expanding network of local schools, to systematize public education much as the factories had been systematized during the industrial revolution.

There are exceptions, to be sure, and these well-run district offices do provide precisely the kind of leadership and originality envisioned. Yet, there is a broad problem, and it may be here, at the district level, where we have the most to learn from our counterparts in England. England, like the United States, has been accustomed to local control, with its local education authorities (LEAs)—the equivalent of school districts—responsible for school budgets, staffing, and the physical plant. But since 1988, when legislation devolved power to each school—school-based management, we'll call it—most administrative decisions have been made by headteachers (principals) and lay representatives who serve as school governors. It's been a remarkable shift in the balance of power, and by most accounts it's been successful.

Such local control has been welcomed by headteachers in England. They report a new sense of energy and control, and of engagement in entrepreneurial activity previously impossible. The school itself can now deploy staff and resources according to its own priorities. Many schools are, in fact, allocating a *higher* percentage of their total budget to the classroom, increasing overall spending on books, computer equipment, and materials, as well as teachers' aides to free teachers from administrative and other duties so that they may actually teach. Perhaps most important, financial independence has boosted morale. School leaders exhibit a genuine sense of pride in their institutions and a collective commitment to the educational mission.

To be sure, the picture hasn't been all rosy. Among the lessons we might learn from England is the need to involve teachers more fully in day-to-day decision making (the findings of Carnegie Foundation teacher surveys have borne this out time and again). The English experience with school autonomy also cautions against headteachers and deputies becoming too preoccupied with financial management—marketing, fundraising, and the like—at the expense of the essential enterprise of teaching and learning. Clearly, a balance must be struck.

But what about the district office? As the power of local schools in England has grown, the role of the local education authorities has shifted, not disappeared. District educators now focus on supporting schools, monitoring their work, and planning for the future. They organize in-service training, coordinate programs for students with special needs, and provide essential services, such as bus transportation. Authorities help schools implement the national curriculum standards and administer the national assessments. Thus schools, once subservient to the local authorities, are now *consumers* of their *services.*

What then about the United States? As we approach a new century, I'm convinced that the governance of American public education must be thoughtfully reexamined. No one wants a Federal ministry of education or national school board to dictate policy for each school. On the other hand, it is equally unacceptable for eighty-three thousand schools to operate in isolation without any sense of overall direction.

I suggest a division of labor. Specifically, I propose a governance arrangement with national goals, statewide standards and accountability for procedures, with much more freedom and budgeting control being given to each local school. The local school should be held accountable for outcomes.

Under this new governance arrangement, the role of the *district* office would be completely overhauled. It would not be one more bureaucratic layer. Borrowing from the English experience, the district role would shift from *administrative control* to *educational enrichment.* District leaders would act as liaisons between state education departments and schools, helping states to set standards and helping schools to interpret and implement them. Districts that connected the various levels of governance—schools, state, and federal—by offering technical assistance would be places that helped, rather than hampered, the cause of reform.

In such a climate, school districts could encourage parents and other community members to become more involved in the local schools. The 1988 Education Reform Act in England, for example, assigned new powers to school governors, many of them parents. The local authorities there offer training courses that help familiarize governors with school finance, accounting, education law, and other aspects of management. Why couldn't our school districts help educate parents about such issues as school finance and standards, to lift the level of local school debates?

District offices of the future also might help schools with curriculum and assessment. In the past, school boards and textbook writers largely determined the curriculum. In this new arrangement, districts could help schools clarify the current curriculum morass, and better still they would consult with schools that wish to raise state standards or tailor them more precisely to local circumstances. In England, districts mount seminars for teachers; one borough built a curriculum library and resource center.

Under the new arrangement, the district office could help schools monitor their educational progress, drawing perhaps upon the British tradition of school "inspection." For example, why couldn't districts assemble teams of professionals and laymen to go inside schools, to ensure that standards are being met and that students are receiving their education in a safe and secure environment?

The district office could also strengthen the education community's commitment to nondiscrimination and equity. It is, after all, the promise of public education to guarantee access for all. Districts eager to serve client schools must not forget their historic commitment to promote fairness. A local school official in England reminds us that local districts must exist to be "orchestrators and securers of fair play."

School choice is another area where the new district office might be especially effective, helping match children to schools based on sound educational criteria, not on gossip, geography, or trivial reasons, as is often the case today. Instead of schools competing with each other for students and the money each brings (a real concern under England's open enrollment and per-capita funding scheme), districts could help assign students, mediate any disputes, and expand the number of successful schools in the local "market." In a 1992 Carnegie special report, *School Choice*, we argue that before choice is introduced, every school in the district must be a school worth choosing. Managing choice in a manner that supplements, rather than supplants, the network of local schools could indeed be one of the most important functions of school districts.

Again, the intention here is not to abolish the large district office. Rather, the goal is to dramatically overhaul the current clumsy structure in which everyone is in charge and yet no one is in charge. The new structure—with national goals, statewide standards, and local control—would empower every principal and teacher and leave them accountable for outcomes, not paperwork and procedures.

I believe all districts—small and large, from Ventura County in California to New York City—would benefit from renegotiating their contract with local schools and performing their duties in a more collegial fashion.

I believe, too, that it's possible for this country to move away from the hierarchical governance arrangement toward a more flexible, albeit tiered, pattern that allows the various levels to operate in concert. States, of course, would still have the authority—and the obligation—to intervene when schools fail, but not before these struggling institutions were given every measure of support to succeed.

Again, let me underscore the point that our current network of school districts is by no means a failure and that not all large districts are ineffective. It is equally important to remember that in focusing especially on the problems of urban districts, we are not talking about a failure of individuals, but rather about failures in the system that stifle creativity and muddle critical issues of authority and accountability. One only has to look at the average tenure of big-city superintendents—less than three years—to see that it's something in the system itself that needs fixing.

HORACE MANN, in his seventh annual report as secretary of the Massachusetts Board of Education, reflects on his itinerant travels to schools throughout Europe: "On the one hand, I am certain that the evils to which our system is exposed, or under which it now labors, exist in some foreign countries in a far more aggravated degree than among ourselves; and if we are wise enough to learn from the experience of others rather than await the infliction consequent upon our own errors, we may yet escape the magnitude and formidableness of those calamities under which some other communities are now suffering. On the other hand, I do not hesitate to say that there are many things abroad which we at home should do well to imitate; things some of which are here, as yet, mere matters of speculation and theory, but which, there, have long been in operation, and are now producing a harvest of rich and abundant blessings."[1]

---

[1] Horace Mann, Seventh Annual Report of the Secretary of the Board, Massachusetts Board of Education, Boston, 1844; reprinted in *Education in the United States: A Documentary History*, vol. 2, Sol Cohen, ed. (New York: Random House, 1974), 1083.

We discovered that there may, indeed, be some aspects of the British reforms worthy of adaptation, if not downright imitation, in the United States. While our country, with its fifty states and large, diverse population, is not inclined toward a national curriculum, we do have national goals and a developing system of statewide standards and assessment programs. There is an abiding interest in school choice. And there is much talk about freeing schools from top-down decision making, allowing them to manage themselves and to be held accountable for the results they achieve.

I am deeply grateful to Kathryn Stearns for so clearly and effectively reviewing the progress and problems English educators have experienced. Most especially, I appreciate the issue she has highlighted about school governance. I am convinced that on this point especially we do have much to learn from colleagues overseas and that we can find the language to redefine how schools in this country are controlled. England, known for centuries for its way with words and more recently for its commitment to innovation in education, might just be the place to turn to learn some important lessons.

SCHOOL REFORM

INTRODUCTION

Snapshots from Abroad

THE INTRODUCTION of a national curriculum has profoundly changed both the politics and the practice of primary and secondary schooling in England and Wales. Our reform-minded tour of England begins with some snapshots to illustrate these changes:

> In a sixth-grade classroom, children are talking about World War II. "Okay, what's VE Day and what's VJ Day?" asks their teacher. Hands fly up. The history lesson is just one of many in the primary years. Schoolchildren between the ages of nine and eleven must also study the Romans, Anglo-Saxons and Vikings, life in Tudor times, Victorian Britain, ancient Greece and a non-European society of the past. The requirement was formulated by the School Curriculum and Assessment Authority and laid down in the National Curriculum Orders.

> Spring is exam time. Around the country, teachers are assessing language skills by using tests authorized by the government. One recent question asked fourteen-year-olds to read act 4, scene 3 of Shakespeare's *Julius Caesar* and to compose an essay on the character of Brutus. This standardized test is typical of many that English and Welsh schoolchildren will take in the core subjects.

What should students know and be able to do? The British government answered that question by designating standards in ten subjects and ordering assessments at regular intervals. Laxity in the classroom, low achievement, and poor workforce-related skills led the country to mandate what teachers should teach and what students should be expected to understand.

What were the social and political arguments used to justify a national curriculum and a system of national assessment? How were they written and implemented? What have been the implications? We looked at the curriculum with these and other questions in mind, believing there are important lessons here for American educators, curriculum specialists, legislators, and other policymakers who are writing frameworks, adopting standards, and developing better methods for monitoring student achievement and comparing school performance.

Two more snapshots:

> Martin Roberts, a principal in Oxford, leads a high school of more than nine hundred pupils, appoints teachers, buys supplies, hires contractors, monitors utilities, and manages a $3 million budget. He is not alone. Most of the twenty-five thousand headteachers in England and Wales deploy staff, allocate resources, and keep their own accounts. School governors—there are approximately 335,000 of them—have overall responsibility for educational and financial planning, but they tend to delegate the day-to-day administration and management to headteachers.
>
> In Birmingham, a group of school governors and parents resolve to "opt out" of their local district and become one of England's first "grant-maintained" schools. Despite a fierce battle waged by the city's chief education officer, the teachers' unions, and members of Parliament, Small Heath wins its bid to become a self-governing institution, severing its administrative and financial ties with the local education authority. Seven years later there are more than one thousand grant-maintained schools receiving funds directly from the central government.

"Local control" has acquired a new connotation in England. Schools have considerable managerial autonomy and administrative flexibility now that the local authorities must delegate operating funds. Local school management has transferred power from the town councillors and district administrators to those most closely affiliated with the schools themselves. Headteachers and school governors largely determine how to spend the money allocated to them.

Small Heath and hundreds of other schools take managerial freedom one step further by exercising their option to "secede" from district control altogether. Grant-maintained schools were created by a government keen to break up the "monopoly" of local schools, shatter administrative complacency, and increase choice within the state sector. Parents dissatisfied with the management of their schools can, by majority vote, wrest them from the local authority.

England's fifteen city technology colleges—newly created schools specializing in applied science—represent a further experiment in self-governance. Like grant-maintained schools, city technology colleges receive funding directly from the central government. In addition, though, they benefit from the financial and promotional support of commercial and industrial sponsors.

What have the new managerial arrangements meant for schools and their local districts? Has financial delegation improved school administration and organization? What is the effect of greater institutional autonomy on the classroom? In this report, we describe England's scheme of local management, and we gauge its impact on various aspects of the education service. We also take a closer look at grant-maintained schools and city technology colleges to see what these new institutions can tell us about the assets and liabilities of self-governance. The English experience offers some useful hints for states and school districts that want to grant principals more flexibility, decentralize their systems, or create charter schools.

Two final snapshots:

> In the auditorium of the Burntwood School, parents gather for an "open evening." To a packed house, teachers and administrators describe the curriculum, extracurricular activities, disciplinary policy, and the admissions procedure. Similar scenes are

repeated throughout assembly halls during the fall season. Selecting a school in England means attending presentations, taking tours, talking to parents, reading brochures, filling out application forms, listing preferences—and playing the odds.

Wright Robinson High School invites prospective students to use its swimming pool, hands out a "starter kit" of pens and pencils, and displays posters about the school in local shops. All this is part of a carefully crafted admissions strategy to lure students into this secondary school outside Manchester. A loss of just ten pupils may mean a budget cut of more than $30,000—enough to wreak havoc with staffing.

Choice and a competitive market underpin compulsory schooling in England. The government was keen to shift influence and control from the education establishment, or the "producers," to parents and other community members, or "consumers." Open enrollment, per-pupil funding, and financial delegation are all strategies intended to empower parents and to make schools more responsive to their preferences. Schools must vie for students and the money each one brings.

What can England's choice plan, with its emphasis on deregulation and financial reward, tell us about choice schemes in the United States and elsewhere? We hope the discussion here adds to what we wrote in a Carnegie Foundation special report called *School Choice,* published in 1992. As we noted then, a scarcity of information too often confounds what has become an ideologically riven debate. England offers a dynamic investigation site from which we can draw additional evidence about the effects of market competition on schools.

Standards, autonomy, and *school choice,* then, are the main issues of this report from England. In the pages that follow, we fill in the background and add some color to the snapshots presented here. Not all the pictures are as rosy as they may first appear. The introduction of the national curriculum and nationally standardized tests resulted in confusion in the classroom, political dissent, and a crippling labor dispute between the government and the teachers' unions. Teachers complained of the curriculum's prescriptive detail and of burdensome tasks associated with assessment. In 1993 and again in 1994, they refused to administer the nationally standardized tests linked to the programs of study. The boycott forced the School Curriculum and Assessment Authority back to the drawing board. A simpler, slimmed-down curriculum was introduced in the fall of the 1995–96 academic year.

At the same time, the law allowing schools to opt out of local control was tantamount to a declaration of war against the education authorities. The hostilities continue today. As the central government wages a fervent campaign to liberate schools from the parochial constraints of the town halls and county councils, the local authorities vigorously defend their territory and maintain a steady counteroffensive. Bids for grant-maintained status have divided communities and set otherwise like-minded educators against one another.

Finally, the government's choice program has charged the atmosphere in which schools operate. In some jurisdictions, there is a scramble for school places; parents too often confuse the right to state a preference and the right to a space at a preferred school. While choice has engaged parents, it has also led to confusion, disappointment, and an explosion of appeals. Schools, forced to behave like small businesses, have become fiercely competitive.

The pictures, good and bad, of school reform that appear in these pages are meant to enliven and enrich the debate about standards, autonomy, and choice in our own country. We use England like a zoom lens, to focus on some of the strategies of interest to U.S. educators, state legislators, and other policymakers just now.

To be sure the lens is imperfect. The snapshots of reform from England can't be superimposed easily onto the U.S. scene. There are, after all, too many differences between the English and U.S. school systems— different histories, different governmental structures, different funding arrangements, different cultures of schooling. Consider, for example, that secondary students in England must earn certificates awarded by independent examinations boards, a longstanding practice that influences the design of curriculum standards and assessments. In the United States, where external examinations are rare and a national curriculum is political anathema, the setting of standards follows a different path. Consider, too, that governing bodies are an old institution in England, though once considerably less powerful than they are today. What would devolution of authority look like where no such tradition exists? Finally, it's important to remember that England does not observe a separation between church and state. Most Anglican, Catholic, and other religious schools receive their funding directly from the central government, and they are, effectively, part and parcel of the state system. That fact dramatically alters the terms of the debate over choice in the two countries.

Still, there are plenty of commonalities, and we believe the English reforms are well worth examining for what they reveal about school improvement. There's hardly a school board or state legislature that hasn't contemplated, at one time or another, raising standards, revising the curriculum, improving assessment, granting more autonomy to individual schools, or widening the boundaries for school choice. This view from England is intended to help guide them in their efforts.

We turn first to the question of standards and the British government's adoption of a national curriculum and a system of assessment.

CHAPTER 1

Standards: Going for Control

THE U.S. REFORM MOVEMENT that began more than a decade ago has a new focal point: the curriculum. Once the province of teachers and textbook writers, the curriculum is now the territory of all who want to broaden the knowledge and improve the skills of American students. The content of classroom work—and how well pupils master that content—concerns not just educators but politicians as well.

Standard-setting has become a national pastime.

Almost every state in the union—forty-nine out of fifty, according to the American Federation of Teachers—is revising standards to focus more on core academic content.[1] More than thirty are linking these standards to performance or "valued outcomes."[2] Oregon and Minnesota have developed "certificates of mastery." While these efforts vary in detail and scope, states have come to recognize that clear expectations for learning and performance are imperative if schoolchildren are to meet the national education goals forged by the governors in 1989.

Meanwhile, curriculum groups have moved swiftly to develop standards in particular subjects; the mathematics standards are already having an impact in a third of the nation's classrooms, according to the National Council of Teachers of Mathematics. Standards in other subjects are being written and argued over, though some efforts are being stalled.

The Goals 2000 legislation, which awards states that establish high standards, was a sign of the times. Though the bill came under fire from the Republican-controlled Congress after the 1994 elections, it exemplified unprecedented national and federal interest in what students should know.

All this recent activity amounts to a revolution in American education.

England's National Curriculum and Its Assessment

Across the Atlantic, there was similar revolution with a decidedly different outcome. The quest for higher standards and more accountable schools led the British government to seize control of the curriculum and all the apparatus used to monitor achievement. The step was radical. No other country in the world has a system that gives such comprehensive control of the curriculum to politicians and civil servants.[3]

How did a country with such strong local traditions come to mandate the "knowledge, skills and understanding" expected of all students? What were the arguments used to justify a national curriculum? To answer these questions it helps to back up to Victorian times, when grants to primary schools depended on pupil performance. "Payment by results" forced teachers to adhere to common standards and fairly uniform lessons. Inspectors chartered by the crown kept tight watch. In the British context, central control and an emphasis on outcomes and accountability aren't entirely new.[4]

By the early twentieth century, however, the local education authorities had assumed responsibility for the schools within their jurisdictions. In practice, headteachers determined the curriculum. At the secondary level, they were influenced by the expectations of the universities and by the requirements of the universities' examinations boards.

During the interwar years, as totalitarian regimes rose to power, central dictates were regarded with deep suspicion. The 1944 Education Act, which established the foundations of England's modern school system, mandated religious instruction but made no other reference to the curriculum. The central ministry was preoccupied with school construction and the recruitment and training of teachers.[5]

After the great expansion of secondary schooling in the fifties and sixties, the curriculum came under government scrutiny once again. Prime Minister James Callaghan called attention to what was taught in the schools—an unusual move for a leading politician in 1976 if not in

1996. The "Great Debate" he launched focused attention directly on teachers' skills and student achievement. The curriculum, sometimes described as the educators' "secret garden," became a matter not just of professional interest but of public and political interest as well. Throughout the seventies and eighties, civil servants disseminated a variety of nonstatutory frameworks intended to help guide the local authorities and the teachers.

Why the sudden interest in what was taught? According to school inspectors, decades of curricular freedom had resulted in an "unacceptable diversity."[6] The calibre of the curriculum depended too much on the calibre of the school and its teachers. Some schools offered a rigorous, well-rounded program to their pupils; too many others provided an inadequate course "menu." As one headteacher put it to us: "Students were spending half a term on the history of Benin and never getting around to the Romans." Many students, particularly girls, failed to receive adequate science instruction, and modern languages had dropped off the list of subjects routinely taught.

The primary curriculum was often criticized as overly "child-centered"—a backlash against a more progressive pedagogy favored by some schools during the late 1960s. A decade later, disillusioned educators and politicians, citing poor literacy skills, were calling for a renewed emphasis on the three Rs.

Forces well outside the schools were also bearing down on policymakers. As in the United States, Britain looked at its economic future and recognized the imperative for well-educated, skilled workers. Once the "workshop of the world," the country had long since lost its competitive edge in manufacturing. Managerial, professional, and technical jobs were beginning to replace manual and machine jobs. Employers demanded graduates who could write well and solve problems.

On this score, there was cause for concern. Achievement overall in England was low. The vast majority of youngsters left school at sixteen, many without the requisite skills. Students weren't measuring up to their European and Asian counterparts; international comparisons, for instance, exposed stark differences among students in comparable countries. One survey carried out in the mid–1960s revealed that the average

English thirteen-year-old lagged a year behind German youngsters and two years behind Japanese youngsters in basic mathematics.[7] Other international indicators pointed to similar weaknesses in achievement.

What did these high-achieving countries have that England did not? The question engaged British educators and social scientists, many of whom advanced a cultural explanation. They characterized British attitudes, particularly among the working classes, as anti-educational. France, Germany, and Japan, by contrast, were thought of as "learning societies." The evidence from these countries suggested that high expectations for all could lead to high achievement. In England, high expectations were reserved for just one segment of the school population—the academic high-flyers and those bound for college and university. The majority quit school at sixteen.

By the late 1980s, the case for the national curriculum had been made. Advocates believed it would: provide a framework for a diverse and divided system; raise expectations and hence achievement; and entice more to stay on in school. While there had been much disagreement on the subject just a few years earlier, there was now a remarkable political consensus that a national curriculum would benefit the nation and improve its economic outlook. According to Michael Barber, who had helped to formulate policy for the National Union of Teachers, there was a kind of national conversion to the idea.[8] The challenge to devise a workable scheme—actual legislation—fell to Margaret Thatcher's Conservative government and to the secretary of state for education, Kenneth Baker.

ANYONE WHO HAS FOLLOWED curriculum writing, whether in the New York City borough of Queens or in California, knows that the exercise is a delicate balance of educational, political, and cultural interests. The devil is in the details. England is no exception. Here, we offer only a synopsis of its development and some of the highlights of more than five years of turmoil and triumph.

The first curriculum was drafted and implemented with remarkable speed. Two years after the parliamentary debates began in the fall of 1987, the core subjects—English, mathematics, and science—were introduced into primary classrooms. Orders for other subjects, including history, geography, and technology, soon followed—a "relentless rolling program," as one teacher described it.

The law establishes that all state schools should have a "balanced and broadly based" curriculum that promotes the "spiritual, moral, cultural, mental and physical development of pupils at the school and of society; and prepare such pupils for the opportunities, responsibilities and experiences of adult life."[9] Beyond these unobjectionable generalities, it identifies a "basic curriculum" to consist of a "national curriculum" and religious education, which was mandated in 1944. The national curriculum's "core" subjects (English, mathematics, and science) are supplemented by seven "foundation" subjects (art, geography, history, modern languages, music, physical education, and technology).

For each of the subjects, the curriculum must:

1) specify "attainment targets," or "the knowledge, skills and understanding which pupils of different abilities and maturities are expected to have by the end of each key stage"—roughly at ages seven, eleven, fourteen, and sixteen;

2) specify the programs of study or "matters, skills and processes which are required to be taught to pupils" at each key stage;

3) and establish "arrangements for assessing pupils at or near the end of each key stage for the purpose of ascertaining what they have achieved in relation to the attainment targets for that stage."

It's important to note that the law does *not* specify how the subjects are to be organized, how much time should be spent on each, the methodologies or the textbooks to be used.

The legislation authorized two new governmental agencies to advise the education secretary on the curriculum and assessment. The agencies have since merged to become the School Curriculum and Assessment Authority, whose members are appointed by the education secretary. The council oversees the appointed working groups, drafts the curriculum and testing orders, consults with the public, and reports to the education ministry. In essence, SCAA is the engine room of the great curricular ship launched in 1988. Grants to the curriculum and assessment councils, as well as money for implementation, amounted to about $61 million in 1994–95.[10] This figure does not include grants for training, which we turn to later.

The law shifts the power over the curriculum from the local education authorities to the central government, or as some have preferred to state the case, from the professionals to the politicians and their appointed representatives. This is not a unique arrangement in the European or Pacific context; in countries as diverse as France, Germany, Sweden, and Japan, central governments exercise varying degrees of control over the curriculum. But in England, the legislative proposal and its accompanying discussion documents sent shock waves through the profession. While there had been general agreement among politicians and policymakers that a national curriculum could lend coherence and lift standards, there was little agreement among the teachers themselves on just what a specific curriculum should entail or on what the secretary of state's role should be. The years of circulars on curricular matters had not prepared most classroom teachers or administrators for the radical changes proposed by the government. In particular, the law gives vast powers to the secretary of state for education, including the right to revise the curriculum, exclude its provisions in certain cases, to require information on particular schools, and so on.

Initial consultations with educators demonstrated the dissent within the ranks. Of more than eleven thousand responses to the government's initial proposal, most expressed reservations about the national curriculum as proposed.[11] This correspondence should have served as a warning sign to the government, but Conservative politicians weren't in the mood for listening. Many blamed the country's poor academic standing on a pervasive laxity within the schools and accused teachers of subordinating children's needs to their own.[12] A drawn-out salary dispute between 1984 and 1987 only served to heighten the animosity between the government and the profession. Public sentiment turned against the teachers as well. "We've had to endure a kind of smear campaign," one teacher told us.

The curriculum written after 1988 reflects the government's uncompromising stance, leading many to complain that it was seeking a "teacher-proof" document. Civil servants opted not for a guiding framework but for a series of precise instructions for each subject. The curriculum authority compiled and distributed thick binders mandating the requirements; the original curriculum led to the creation of some one thousand "statements of attainment" describing the knowledge or skills expected of students at various stages.

Much of the curriculum's complexity resulted from the complexity of the testing program, which we describe in more detail in the next section. Why? Because once the government decided to compile data on the achievement of students in various subjects at various ages, it was necessary to enumerate exactly what they should achieve, and to what levels.

A brief description of the early science curriculum illustrates the prescriptive nature of the program. The curriculum specified four attainment targets: scientific investigation, life and living processes, materials and their properties, and physical processes. These targets are then described at ten levels. At level one, the curriculum required students to: observe familiar materials and events; be able to name or label the main external parts of the body and a flowering plant; know that there is a wide variety of living things; describe simple properties of familiar materials; know that many household appliances use electricity but that misuse is dangerous; understand that things can be moved by pushing or pulling them; know about the simple properties of sound and light; and be able to describe the apparent movement of the sun across the sky. The curriculum then progresses up nine more levels. Mature students are expected to use and understand scientific laws, theories, and models, collect data, comprehend homeostatic and metabolic processes, know what DNA is, recognize chemical reactions, and so forth.

The scheme of progression and the ten-level scale to which it is calibrated—both linked to the assessment program—have generated controversy. The objective was to provide an intelligible means of reporting pupils' skills, but it has confounded teachers and parents alike. Some subjects, such as science and mathematics, lend themselves more readily to a system of progression than others, such as English and history. In addition, the design has led to anomalies. Parents ask how both a seven-year-old and a fourteen-year-old can score at level three.[13] While some have found the scale transparent, others complain that it, like the curriculum itself, is too cumbersome. Teachers, required by law to record and report what each student had achieved, were expected to make lengthy checklists, ticking off each statement of attainment as it was mastered.

A curriculum needn't be so complicated. The French curriculum is described in a single pamphlet. Just what to include in England's was the subject of a sharp political debate dividing the Conservative Party. Keith Joseph, education secretary in the mid-1980s, was keen to see higher standards and a basic curriculum but not a prescriptive program. An influential Conservative think tank, the Centre for Policy Studies, urged a core curriculum in English, mathematics, and science—a model Prime Minister Margaret Thatcher preferred.

But others, including education secretary Kenneth Baker, insisted that standards wouldn't rise unless the government imposed a broader curriculum that exposed students to many academic subjects and a larger range of experiences. This faction held sway. Baker writes: "The whole purpose of a curriculum is that it sets out in detail the progressive growth in knowledge which a child has to experience. Vagueness and lack of detail will allow an inadequate and lazy teacher to skip important parts."[14]

The subject specialists assigned to the working groups took up the ministry's call for specificity and speed. No time was wasted; the core programs—English, math, and science—were written in a matter of months, as was the advisory document on testing. The rapid-fire recommendations were remarkable in the face of the predictable doctrinal and pedagogical disputes, many of which continue today. Should the government require children to memorize poetry, read Shakespeare, adhere to standard English? Should youngsters take one or two sciences? Should children recite the multiplication tables, or resort to calculators? How much history should be British history? Successive education secretaries, permitted by law to modify the curriculum, intervened. One fired committee heads whose suggestions he disapproved and amended orders as he saw fit. To the teachers' dismay, this was proof that the curriculum was to be a political document after all.

The hasty execution of the orders proved yet another folly. Much of the curriculum written in 1989 and 1990 had to be amended even before the wholesale revisions of 1994. The National Curriculum Council, which had several chairmen in several years, was constantly reissuing orders or threatening to. Revisions were made to the English, mathematics, science, and technology curricula. In the case of mathematics and science, the attainment targets were greatly reduced. The effect was destabilizing and produced much confusion and anger among teachers attempting to cope with implementation.

"The main problem has been the constant changes. . . . Schools aren't London taxis," K. H. Brooke, a headteacher in Berkshire, told us.

"Looking back, we didn't realize what a huge monster was unleashed upon us," Brigid Beattie, of the Burntwood School, said. The curriculum and testing councils were like "First World War generals shouting orders."

According to most headteachers we interviewed, staff members attempted as best they could to implement the changes. "If teachers are told to do something, they do it," K. H. Brooke said. But by the spring of 1993, just as the curriculum was beginning to have an impact on secondary schools, teachers (with the full support of parents and headteachers) refused to administer the standardized tests intended for seven- and fourteen-year-olds. The teachers rapped the government for producing assessments that were poorly written and too time-consuming to administer. The boycott of the tests was effectively a boycott of the curriculum itself, and the action amounted to civil disobedience on a national scale. The government was powerless to stop it.

A CURRICULUM DISCARDED by teachers and parents alike is of no use. At the government's behest, the School Curriculum and Assessment Authority conducted a critical review in 1993–94, gathering hours of testimony from teachers and administrators, who emphasized that the curriculum was unmanageable and overly prescriptive. The government thus agreed to reduce the volume of required material, to make more room for professional judgment by reducing the mandates, and to ensure that the orders are written in a way that offers maximum support to the classroom teacher.[15] The government also acknowledged the demoralizing effect of the frequent changes, promising no more revisions for five years once schools adopted the new curriculum in the fall of 1995.

After years of political myopia and bureaucratic bungling, the government learned the hard way the importance of collaborating with the teacher corps. In the words of Sir Ron Dearing, who as chairman of the School Curriculum and Assessment Authority played a vital mediating role: "We have much to learn from the problems teachers have experienced in administering the reforms. We can do a better job."[16] Perhaps most important, classroom teachers now play key roles on the curriculum advisory committees.

The School Curriculum and Assessment Authority was also forced to make procedural changes. During the initial drafting, advisory groups worked in isolation, each claiming a large slice of the curriculum pie. No one teacher, particularly an elementary school teacher, could cover it all. The government conceded the point when it concluded: "The core and foundation subjects as defined through the statutory orders were never intended to absorb virtually all the teaching time available. The orders have, however, been devised individually and at different times by subject specialists who were naturally keen to see that their subject was well covered. The consequence is that there is little scope for teaching outside the national curriculum or for a school to draw upon the particular expertise of its teachers and the opportunities provided by its local environment."[17]

A member of the curriculum authority acknowledged that the challenge in revising the curriculum was "not to separate the bits," to plan the whole of the national curriculum by making sure the subject advisory groups don't convene again in isolation as they did after the law was passed. Many teachers pointed out that cross-curricular themes had been missed by the government, and that the subject-by-subject approach had led to a kind of atomization.

"Each subject working party built up its own piece of the jigsaw," one principal told us. "No one thought to look at the whole or even whether it fit onto the table."

Since September 1995, the statutory curriculum has focused on the core subjects of English, mathematics, and science. Teachers now have more discretionary time for lessons and concentrate more on teaching than on testing. Disputes, of course, continue. Some, for instance, fear that allowing high school students to pick and choose subjects after age fourteen will cheat them once again of a full range of academic programs. Others worry that an emphasis on core subjects diminishes the importance of history, social sciences, and the arts. But most believe the government took a necessary and appropriate step by streamlining the statutory programs and by leaving more of the details to the teachers themselves.

The introduction of the national curriculum required training on a massive scale. The job fell to the local education authorities, principals, department heads, and the teachers themselves. Self-help was common. There wasn't much time to prepare; statutory orders in the core subjects were published in March 1989 for implementation in primary schools in September 1989. "Teacher training was pretty hectic," one headteacher told us.

According to an inspectors' report issued in 1990, "Schools were faced with a difficult task. There was much to be done in a short time. This led to some uncertainty and anxiety. Hard work and professionalism by the providers and teachers meant that, despite some difficulties in organizing the provision, the training received by most teachers was satisfactory or better."[18]

Still, teachers remember the confusion. Was training their responsibility, the local authorities', or the central government's? The curriculum was installed at a time when new governmental relationships within the education service were also taking hold. The National Curriculum Council offered information packs and general guidance, but it was up to schools to find their own way.

The local authorities adopted various strategies, from full-day courses for teachers to a series of meetings over weeks. Some trained all the teachers, others trained those who could then train others. In certain cases, the sessions revealed the need to strengthen teachers' own skills. Many lacked knowledge, for example, in the teaching of science and history.

There has been a scramble for resources as well. With the exception of specific grants for education support and training (which amounted to $232 million in 1994–95), local education authorities (LEAs) had few extra funds to implement the curriculum.[19] Wherever we went, headteachers complained of the hidden costs. Elementary schools, in particular, require more equipment and textbooks for subjects formerly neglected, such as science, history, geography, and technology. Materials for the teaching of geography, for example, were lacking in three-quarters of the elementary schools when that subject was introduced.[20] In Leicestershire, the lack of resources had more stunning consequences. One primary school closed voluntarily because it couldn't afford to deliver the requisite programs. The school merged with another, thereby creating a larger and more economical unit capable of meeting the curriculum's demands.

The costs of the national curriculum—in training, resources, and equipment—are substantial, and they tend to lag behind implementation. According to one estimate, schools needed to spend more than $300 per pupil per year until the necessary adjustments and conversions were made. The direct costs in primary schools were estimated at more than $150 per pupil per year in the first five years.[21]

A typical two-hundred-pupil primary school adequately staffed before the introduction of the national curriculum needed after its introduction one extra full-time teacher and more money to pay allowances to those teachers who took on more specialized duties. Yet few primary schools could afford to hire more teachers; a number of schools, in fact, were forced to increase class size. The national curriculum, in combination with formula funding based on pupil numbers, has caused a severe budget squeeze in many schools.

WE COME TO THE CRUCIAL QUESTION: Can a national curriculum raise standards and improve student achievement? In England's case, the curriculum and its assessment are too new and too unstable to say anything definitive. There are both encouraging signs and warning signs.

According to the country's chief inspector of schools, "a number of clear improvements can be seen from the gradual—though not untroubled and as yet incomplete—introduction of the national curriculum."[22] Seven-year-olds performed slightly better in 1992 on assessments in major subjects than they did in 1991.

Certain improvements are apparent. In the primary schools, there is now a more varied curriculum—though most teachers find it difficult to introduce all the national curriculum subjects and to assess children so young. Most primaries continue to focus on literacy and numeracy skills, but other lessons, by law, are finding their way into the day's schedule. The national curriculum "has led to steady improvement in planning, a better focus on the knowledge, skills and understanding to be taught and a more secure place in the curriculum for science, technology, history and geography," according to inspectors.[23]

In one large village primary we visited, a classroom teacher was leading eleven- and twelve-year-olds in a discussion of World War II. "Okay, what's VE Day and what's VJ Day?" he asked. Models of air raid shelters were displayed on tables in the hallway. This is one lesson, the principal admitted, that wouldn't have been attempted before the imposition of the national curriculum.

Though many argue that a ten-subject curriculum is nonsense for children as young as five, others concede primary schools were ignoring too much. "I would regret a cutting back of the national curriculum in primary schools," Ann Sofer, a chief education officer in London's inner city, told a group of educators in the fall of 1993. "The curriculum is more than the three Rs."

Still, the delivery of the national curriculum has not been easy. The gain for science and history, for example, has come at the expense of more traditional subjects. Primary schools have been spending less time on English, mathematics, physical education, art, craft, and music—the staples of an elementary education. Schools are looking to recover time not only for the basics but for the activities that nourish children's imaginations. The slimming down of the national curriculum should help teachers reconcile its demands.

There are other concerns: The pressure to introduce many subjects has forced teachers to return to traditional methods. According to one study, teachers who once enjoyed the flexibility to help individual pupils are now having to address the entire class. Some experts warn that the shift to whole-class teaching will hinder the development of skills gained in group activities, such as problem solving.[24] Teachers are also finding it more difficult to concentrate on topical work emphasizing cross-curricular themes, such as projects on the environment or the weather, for example. The government's subject-by-subject approach frustrates many primary school teachers, though there is no law against teachers taking a multidisciplinary approach.

So far, the national curriculum has yet to eliminate the stark differences among elementary schools, where there continue to be unacceptable variations among schools in similar circumstances and among pupils of similar abilities.[25] But the curriculum has raised the profile of primary education generally, which in the past has tended to receive less attention and less money than the secondary sector.[26]

The curriculum's impact at the secondary level is harder to gauge. It arrived on secondary doorsteps later than on primary ones and was suspended before syllabuses in all ten subjects were distributed in all upper grades. Nevertheless, inspectors again observe improvements and report that the vast majority of secondary schools are successfully providing a "broad and balanced curriculum."[27] Science and modern foreign languages are finding their way back into the timetable. Brigid Beattie told us: "There has been an improvement of learning and that mythical thing called 'standards'—though it's difficult to say it."

For other secondary teachers, however, the national curriculum fixed something that wasn't broken. "After six years of considerable acrimony, Ron Dearing (chairman of the School Curriculum and Assessment Authority) has restored our curriculum to the way it was," Martin Roberts, of the Cherwell School in Oxford, told us. He doubts whether it has raised standards, but he does note that parents, students, and teachers are working together better and that there's been a national mood shift. "A national curriculum five through sixteen seems to make an enormous amount of sense—if you get it right," he said.

The challenge ahead is to integrate the national curriculum with the mixed bag of certification schemes on offer post-sixteen. English students, unlike their American counterparts, must strive for specific academic and/or vocational awards. The "A-levels" are the favored academic qualifications required by the universities. The government has also launched a vocational award program. The independent examinations boards and such validating bodies as the Business and Technology Education Council, the Royal Society for the Encouragement of Arts, Manufactures and Commerce (RSA), and City and Guilds will continue to retain a powerful influence on the courses offered in secondary schools and in the burgeoning further education colleges, which cater to students who have completed their compulsory schooling. Will the national curriculum help to clarify the choices students must make or will it only serve to constrict them? Martin Roberts frames the question slightly differently: "Will teachers feel too constrained to teach well?" The answers to these questions lie in the future.

The introduction of the national curriculum has been politically divisive and pedagogically difficult, yet few would abolish it. After five years, the government is learning to trust the teachers, and the teachers are coming to accept, even to like, a national curriculum. In fact, teachers think the curriculum has done more than any other reform to raise standards.[28] That's a sign that the government's program, recently rewritten more closely to teachers' specifications, has a good chance of success.

In the months following the much-publicized test boycott, we didn't expect teachers to mount a defense of the government's program and perogatives, but most did. Despite the evident frustration with the curriculum authority's heavy-handed approach and its insistence on statutory detail, most educators agree that a national curriculum can help rather than hinder them and their students.

It's important to remember that the national curriculum, while prescriptive, is not a day-by-day lesson plan. Secondary teachers tend to adapt the material as they wish, when they wish, using the resources particular to their schools as well as national curriculum texts. Hence, at the micro level, the national curriculum is experienced differently by pupils in different schools.[29] Committing a set of standards and skills to paper has not led to the often caricatured (and apocryphal) French model that has all students of the same age learning the same lesson at the same time.

One secondary school administrator in London made a telling comment: "There's more fuss made about the national curriculum than there should be. The amount of content is enormous—and about time too!" Many have come to think of the additional course material as a "right of access" for young people. Indeed, England's national curriculum is now regarded as an entitlement. One teacher we met, echoing scores of others, called it "a right for children."

Against all odds, the curriculum seems to be succeeding. It is associated with educational excellence, equity in the classroom, and sound democratic principles. Even the harshest critics concede that a carefully crafted national curriculum can serve a useful purpose and that all citizens have vital roles to play in helping to formulate standards.

WHAT CAN THE UNITED STATES learn from all this? Those seeking to articulate standards in the United States would do well to avoid the political miscalculations and procedural mistakes that marred the introduction of a national curriculum in England. Above all else, curriculum writers, whoever they are and wherever they may be, must carry the teaching profession along with them. In England, teachers were left behind. The first national curriculum, contained in ten volumes and more than three hundred pages, was not the creation of those who spend their working lives in the classroom. It was the creation of partisan politicians, civil servants, consultants, and academicians.

Denis Lawton, educator and academician, writes: "There is a mass of literature showing that successful curriculum change should start from the professional concerns of teachers, making use of their knowledge and experience, not as a top-down plan imposed on teachers by civil servants.[30] The British government's approach proves the point.

As curriculum associations, school districts, and statehouses throughout the United States assemble committees to establish standards and revise frameworks, it's well to remember that a curriculum is like a script. Politicians and their representatives can contribute to its production, but it is for teachers and students to speak the parts. It is they who must engage in the conversation that is learning.

We glean another, less cautionary lesson. A national curriculum—in America's case, the setting of voluntary national standards—can lend rigor to the profession. Evidence in England abounds that the national curriculum has spurred schools to examine course content more closely and to assess what students are actually learning. Is the balance right? Is each subject covered in sufficient depth? Are teachers adequately trained? In many cases, the curricular reforms imposed by the central government have led individual schools to reform themselves from within.[31]

Can content and performance standards accomplish similar goals throughout the diverse school districts of the United States? We think they can, if there is a broad consensus about what those standards should be, and if the standards are truly dynamic. American teachers and students need to know what's expected of them. High standards, fairly formulated and clearly articulated, would supply a common language for the vigorous conversation we have in mind for educators, students, parents, and policymakers in this country.

Assessment

Almost inseparable from the national curriculum is the mechanism invented to monitor its success: national testing. England's assessment program, like its curriculum, has fostered fundamental changes in classroom practice, political discontent, and parental confusion.

Until recently, the government did not attempt to collect data on the progress of the majority of pupils in state schools. Instead, student achievement was measured at the end of compulsory schooling, using tests written and administered by independent examinations boards. These tests have changed over the years, but their primary purpose was, and continues to be, to certify students and to rank and sort those bound for post-secondary education.

The Education Reform Act added considerably to the testing burden by instituting assessments at various ages in an attempt to monitor standards nationwide. In addition to the certifying exams at sixteen, the law mandated tests of seven-, eleven-, and fourteen-year-olds as well. The legislation specified nothing about the kinds of tests that were to be used. But the government made clear that the stakes were high. Students were to be assessed in order to monitor their progress, aid teaching, compare performance among schools, and promote accountability. Test scores were to become the common currency in the new education marketplace, a way of determining a school's worth.

The assessment scheme recommended in 1988 by the Task Group on Assessment and Testing (TGAT) was a dramatic departure from previous, national-scale proposals. It consisted of two components: 1) continuous teacher assessment, in which teachers would measure pupils' progress against the national curriculum's "attainment targets"; and 2) external standardized tests, supplied by the government, that would satisfy the public's demand for accountability. Experts envisioned a seamless integration of teaching, learning, and assessment based on standards, or agreed-upon performance criteria. Paul Black, of the University of London and chairman of the task group, writes: "The central purpose was to respect and strengthen pupils' learning and teachers' professional role, whilst at the same time supporting tough and valid assessment to satisfy the legitimate demands of public accountability. The outcome was very ambitious."[32]

The members of the panel, who designed the assessment program in a few short months, wanted to avoid the pitfalls of the well-documented American experience with multiple-choice testing, including the tests' tendency to "dumb down" the curriculum. Instead, the task force looked to the best practices of England's examinations boards, which routinely ask students to submit essays, portfolios, and answers to mathematical and scientific problems. The experts also borrowed from the burgeoning research file on alternative assessment.

Pencil-and-paper tests, in other words, were not what the task group had in mind. Instead, the group recommended "standard assessment tasks" (SATs) that would resemble carefully designed classroom activity. The tasks would be similar in schools across the country but graded by the teachers themselves according to common performance criteria. The task force encouraged oral, written, and pictorial work; practical demonstrations; and the use of computers. In theory, young students wouldn't necessarily know they were being tested.

The results of the teachers' own assessments and those for the standardized tasks were to be combined by using a process known as "group moderation," which requires the teachers themselves to discuss the work, compare it, and make a judgment about it—a time-consuming and expensive process. But teachers in England are familiar with the practice, because the public examinations require moderators.

The task force was wary of using the scores for purposes of comparison. It recommended that the results for seven-year-olds should not be published; that individual results should be for parents and pupils only; that school scores should be published only if accompanied by a full report on the school and its population; and finally, that the scheme should be implemented over five years, with sufficient research and development and, most important, teacher training.

Actual practice soon strayed from the specific recommendations. For reasons both political and practical, the immensely complex and innovative model devised by the task group wasn't implemented. Though the government concurred with the experts' framework, it ignored some of the most crucial advice contained in the report—namely, the need for careful research and development, teacher training, adequate resources, and the importance of respecting teachers' own judgments.

Technical obstacles impaired the program. As we've noted, the curriculum writers made a nonsense of assessment by loading down each subject with too many attainment targets. How could a primary teacher efficiently monitor progress on thirty-two criteria contained in the core curriculum? Later, the number of attainment targets, necessary for criterion-referencing, had to be whittled down.

Further, the balance between teacher assessment and national assessment tilted. The government, which little valued or understood the teachers' role in assessing their students, placed a greater emphasis—and more money—on the standardized examinations. Teacher assessments were demoted, and professional development for group moderation was abandoned.

The first national assessments were conducted in 1991 on children seven years old. Youngsters were asked to read aloud, for example, or use dice to play mathematics games or sort objects. The testing methods, in short, were consistent with good classroom practice.[33] But the exercise proved difficult for the primary teachers, who weren't accustomed to administering such performance-based assessments and reporting the results. The preparation, administration, and marking gobbled up classroom time. Administration alone took at least forty hours for an elementary class of twenty-five to thirty, according to one estimate.[34] Teachers' aides and parent volunteers were required to help administer the exams and attend to those children who weren't being tested. Discipline was sometimes a problem, and most teachers reported severe stress and strain.

Teachers worried about the grading and the comparability of the test results as well. Though the tasks themselves were standardized, the conditions under which the students were examined were not. Some teachers administered the tests in familiar classrooms; others didn't. Some teachers prepared their students as best they could; others disguised the tests, calling them "experiments" or "games."

The media seized on the teachers' complaints, and soon the politicians, including the prime minister, promised simpler standardized tests. Overlooked was the fact that many welcomed the tests, believing that they fostered good and innovative teaching. Preliminary research indicates that by no means all effects of the novel assessments had been bad.

Caroline Gipps, of the University of London's Institute of Education, worked intensively with thirty-two schools in four different districts. She and fellow researchers found that the assessments forced teachers to discuss student performance, broadened their outlook, and improved the quality of their teaching. Administering and grading the standardized assessment tasks had an in-service training effect, according to Gipps' survey. Further, many children enjoyed the tasks.

Significantly, the standardized tasks for seven-year-olds took half the time to administer in 1992, suggesting that the objectionable workloads had decreased, and that teachers had learned to incorporate the assessments into their school day. But in the name of simplicity and savings, the government is moving away from performance tasks and is coming to rely on more conventional tests to assess achievement at each "key stage" of the curriculum.

According to surveys, the other, ostensibly more important, component of the assessment system—teacher assessment—was neglected. Teachers were expected to assess each child against every attainment target identified in the core subjects, but most didn't bother to monitor the progress of their pupils, collect the data, and record it for the government. Those who did attempt to keep records encountered administrative obstacles. Many schools resorted to making lengthy checklists. The mechanics interfered with teaching and learning. In the words of one headteacher: "Teachers tried their best, but they spent all their time doing a tick list and not teaching."

As successive subjects of the national curriculum were introduced, and attainment targets accumulated, the burdens of testing and recording grew unbearable. The 1993 boycott of the standardized assessment tasks was the ultimate expression of the teachers' frustrations with the assessment program.

The government has now decided to focus national tests on the core subjects only, cut the time required for the tests by roughly half, and relieve teachers of unnecessary recordkeeping and form-filling. School performance tables—the comparative listings—will be based on the standardized examinations taken at age eleven.

While many met these developments with a sense of relief, some testing experts remain dismayed. Paul Black, who helped conceive the original scheme, sees danger in a return to unimaginative drills and pencil-and-paper tests. The technical aspects of performance-based assessment aren't publicly understood, he contends. How, he asks, can educators and politicians communicate effectively the strengths and weaknesses of various forms of assessment?

This is a crucial question for the United States, where localities and states are trying to foster better testing practices and where there is a lively debate under way about the desirability of some sort of national achievement examination or examinations. England's run at performance assessment on a national scale hints at the difficulties. The tests aren't easy to produce, cheap to administer, or simple to grade. Teachers, especially those in the primary schools, resented the administrative burden imposed by the design of the assessment program and the time wasted in the classroom. Technical problems aside, they criticized the tests themselves. The teachers of English protested vociferously about what the government was asking of students. Their voices were heard above all others during the 1993 boycott of the tests designed for six hundred thousand students age fourteen.

Finally, there was—and continues to be—widespread confusion and disagreement about the purposes of the standardized tests. Teachers aren't against tests that will help them measure a student's progress and identify weaknesses. What they don't like are tests used to compare school performance, especially when the government intends to report the scores without accompanying details about a school's resources or the children's socioeconomic background.

It's apparent now that the assessment program conceived by government advisers was overly ambitious. It was formulated with too many purposes in mind, from providing teachers with detailed information about their students to providing parents and the government with an indicator of school effectiveness. The notion that *one* program of assessment can fulfill multiple functions has been proved false.[35]

In the United States, the "testing culture" is entirely different from that of England. Basic-skills testing predominates, and the scores are used most often to rank students rather than to improve their skills or assist teachers. Aptitude tests used widely for college admission don't assess mastery of subject matter. The United States has yet to develop the kinds of complex assessment and accountability systems common to other countries in Europe and Asia.[36]

But the aims of testing, along with the designs of the tests themselves, are beginning to change. Alternative assessments that require students to write essays, make mathematical computations, conduct science experiments, present oral arguments, or assemble portfolios are becoming more commonplace. California has introduced tests that rely on written answers to questions about literature and other subjects. In Vermont, teachers are learning to evaluate portfolios of students' work. The New Standards Project, a joint initiative of the National Center on Education and the Economy and the University of Pittsburgh, is working with school districts to develop examinations tied to curriculum standards. If these tests of performance are to become useful diagnostic tools and measurements of achievement, then teachers, politicians, and parents must understand and support the instruments, concur with their purpose, and bear the cost.

CHAPTER II

Autonomy: Going It Alone

ONE OF THE MOST SENSITIVE ISSUES facing reformers in America now is the question of how to manage and govern the public schools. School boards and district superintendencies have stood the nation in good stead for more than a century, but the years have brought stunning changes. School districts are larger, more diverse, and beset with far more social and economic problems than they were one hundred years ago, when lay boards were installed to oversee village schools. The country's largest urban systems are under siege, fighting financial, social, and political crises. The challenges can overwhelm even the most able administrators; the average tenure for superintendents in the country's largest metropolitan districts is less than three years. The instability leads to the dangerous conclusion that the most troubled districts, with America's neediest students, can't—or won't—be governed.

Schools, for their part, complain of bureaucratic interference and unnecessary regulations. Too often, the central office acts as an obstructionist rather than as a facilitator. Principals seek flexibility and managerial "wiggle room." District 4 in New York City, famous for its program of school choice, has made a name for itself in part by fighting for waivers from state and local rules.

Frustration with administration and management has led to an evident impatience with the status quo. In recent years, for example, maverick legislators have proposed everything from allowing schools to secede from their districts to the abolition of school boards altogether. A few districts, including those in Florida, Maryland, Massachusetts, Minnesota, and New Jersey, have turned their schools over to private management consultants. The growing movement to create "charter schools" is yet another indication that politicians are seeking a new model for school management.

There are less radical approaches. For years, many districts have been delegating more responsibility to those at the school site. School-based management (sometimes called school-site management) has become a favored strategy across America. Chicago is conducting one of the nation's boldest experiments in decentralization. There, each school elects its own local council, which has the authority to hire and fire the principal, develop the budget, and plan capital improvements. In Kentucky, a statewide reform effort requires all schools to have a governing council by 1996. Some of these councils have already convened, and they are making important decisions on staffing, curriculum, and other policies.[1] Countless other districts, from Dade County, Florida, to Moses Lake, Washington, are yielding more control to those within the schools.

But school-based management continues to be regarded as an experimental strategy rather than as a conventional one. Districts that do delegate managerial and budgetary responsibilities tend to do so halfheartedly or temporarily.

LOCAL MANAGEMENT IN ENGLAND

In England, by contrast, local management is the law. Budgets once guarded by the local education authorities have been devolved to the school heads and governors, who make most of the decisions that directly affect the classroom, whether that decision is to employ more teachers' aides or to buy more xylophones for the music room. Leaky roofs get fixed faster—and often for less money—than they used to. In fact, financial delegation has remedied many of the problems associated with unresponsive and distant bureaucracies.

That, of course, was the point. Local management shifted the decision-making power from more than one hundred regional districts to tens of thousands of headteachers and governing bodies—a stunning realignment in a country that, like the United States, was accustomed to local district control. Previously, the local education authorities determined staffing and met basic costs. Now they must yield to the smaller managerial teams within the schools themselves. Headteachers and governors have assumed a host of important duties, from appointing teachers to buying textbooks and maintaining buildings and grounds. The administrative transfer, long sought by many school heads, has led to greater flexibility and more effective management.

Why did the government propose such a bold strategy? Certainly the Conservatives were drawn to the doctrine of local management. The education authorities, in their view, were spendthrifts. Why not let individual schools keep their own budgets, determine staffing levels and, like businesses, adhere to sensible accounting practices? In short, local management would compel school administrators to be efficient and to look at the bottom line. It would also force headteachers to become more responsible—spending decisions, after all, would have to be justified to school governors and to parents.

But the government was drawn to something else as well: the potential of local management to sap the considerable political power of the LEAs, many of them controlled by the opposition Labor Party. Hence the charge that local management of schools (LMS) worked its way into the 1988 Education Reform Act not because it would improve schools and their administration but because it would serve to undermine the local politicians.[2]

Others cynically contend that local management was simply a strategy to absolve the central government of responsibility for the schools, to shift the blame from the Department for Education and members of Parliament to the hundreds of thousands of citizens who serve as school governors.

Whatever the political motivation, local management has altered relationships within the English and Welsh education service—for the better, most would agree. For this reason, it is one of the most far-reaching reforms, though it receives far less attention than the national curriculum. Its relevance for the United States lies not only in its power to rearrange managerial hierarchies but in its more humble power to transform the day-to-day, nuts-and-bolts operation of each school. The headteachers we met exercise options they didn't have before, engage in entrepreneurial activity and, most important, describe a high degree of job satisfaction. It is in this context that LMS has worked best—despite the considerable complications caused by the per-capita funding formula designed to trigger a competitive schools market. "I'm a convert to LMS," said Stephen Szemerenyi, head of a Catholic high school in London. "Schools shouldn't blithely carry on without knowing what education costs."

"LMS is here to stay," predicted K. H. Brooke, a secondary headteacher in suburban Berkshire.

Local management of schools wasn't a parliamentary invention. Managerial reforms were on educators' agendas long before the government grabbed hold of the idea. Local authorities throughout the country had been experimenting with devolved budgets and financial decision making at the school site well before the 1988 reforms. In fact, the success of various pilot projects demonstrated the potential of local management.

Interestingly, one of the most closely watched pilot programs emphasized neither economy nor accountability. Cost-cutting was not a primary aim of the financial management scheme introduced in Cambridgeshire in 1982. Rather, the county was seeking the most effective use of resources and more flexibility for headteachers.[3] Schools were allowed to spend their allocated funds as they saw fit. If they realized savings, good. If not, it hardly mattered; next year's budget, based on the budgets of past years, would remain about the same.

The reforms of the 1988 act, however, removed such predictability. No local management scheme, whether districtwide or nationwide, can exist for long without a readily understandable formula for distributing the money. In England, the government discounted a school's "historical" costs and the seemingly arbitrary funding patterns of the LEAs. Instead, it devised a more transparent and supposedly objective formula based on pupil numbers.

It's difficult to disentangle local management from this per-capita budget calculation, open enrollment, and the government's program to promote school choice (to which we turn in the next section). The freedom headteachers ostensibly have to manage school funds is limited by an unforgiving formula engineered to reward those schools that attract the most students. Enrollment figures largely determine each school's budget share. School funding depends almost entirely on the decisions parents make and, of course, on demography. Money follows the child.

Local management, then, is a boon in the growing schools. It is irrelevant in the schools suffering declines, where there is little discretionary money to manage. Educators throughout England note a growing divide between the well-endowed schools and the less well endowed.[4] "I've relished LMS," a primary headteacher in Eastbourne told us, "because I've been a winner. Equally keen heads haven't had the leeway, haven't had the resources to do what they wanted to do . . . and all because of the vagaries of the formula." A secondary headteacher in Oxfordshire was dismissive of LMS. "It hasn't changed the way we've operated," he said. "If we'd been a growing school, our experience would have been different." Said a third: "LMS makes us a lot poorer. We can now choose what not to spend our money on."[5] These comments are an important reminder that LMS is *not* a funding strategy. It is an administrative strategy, and it has been most effective in schools where headteachers and governors can concentrate on education rather than on the economics of survival.

How do the schools get their money? How is the formula derived? Expenditure on primary and secondary education includes grants from the central government (about 80 percent of the total) as well as revenue raised locally, which is subject to caps. Local authorities determine their own education budgets and monitor spending.

Schemes for local management begin with the authorities' "general schools budget." By law, they must retain central government grants for specific purposes (special and bilingual education, for instance) and money for capital expenditures. The statute also specifies a number of services, such as home-to-school transportation, that authorities may continue to provide. The authority must delegate to the schools at least 85 percent of the general schools budget less expenditures on these "excepted" items.

Determining a proportion of the general budget to be delegated wasn't easy, either politically or practically. The government enlisted the help of the accounting firm Coopers and Lybrand Deloitte, which offered a primer on the subject. But it was up to legislators to define the parameters—just what should LEAs continue to pay for and to provide? Government regulations list the specific requirements. It then falls to the LEAs to devise their own specific delegation schemes, within national guidelines and subject to the education secretary's approval. In the first years of local management, authorities exercised considerable discretion, retaining money for such expenditures as curriculum development, guidance counseling, and school lunches. This displeased the government, which wanted to see more money in the schools' hands. So by 1991, it issued new rules that restricted more severely the services the LEAs can provide.

Nor was it easy to devise a formula for allocating the budget into shares for individual schools—the "resource allocation formula." The government sought something "simple, clear and predictable,"[6] but differences among LEAs, among schools, and among students guaranteed complexity. Secondary pupils cost more to educate than primary ones; students with special needs cost more than others; maintenance costs differ; social circumstances vary; and so forth. A formula based *entirely* on pupil numbers wouldn't be fair. Again, LEAs exercise a bit of discretion here, with most taking into account the age, abilities and the overall socioeconomic profile of the students in particular schools. The per-capita calculation is a weighted one, in other words, with an expectation that at least 80 percent of a school's budget will be allocated on the basis of pupil numbers. This has led to continuing variations in funding not only among LEAs but also among similar schools within an LEA. Wide discrepancies in per-pupil costs continue to exist. It's important to remember that the effect of local management depends not only on a school's enrollment but also on the basic level of funding each receives.

Finally, the resource allocation formula disregards a crucial variable: teachers' salaries and other staffing costs. On average, 70 percent or more of a school's budget goes directly to pay salaries, insurance, and related employment expenses. Yet the government rejected any compensatory mechanism for schools that employ more experienced and therefore more expensive teachers. LEAs must calculate each school's budget share by using a national average salary figure rather than the actual figures. The result has been that: a) schools with more experienced teachers have considerably less money, or b) schools have been forced to hire less experienced teachers to save money. The adverse effects of this policy—including an overall rise in the pupil/teacher ratio, according to the Audit Commission—are the source of frustration for educators and local politicians alike. In Birmingham, a city councillor described the case of two otherwise similar primary schools: one that has plenty of resources and a young staff and another that has little money for materials but an experienced staff. "You're penalized for high-quality staffing, experienced teachers," he said.

How schools derive their money is, in the end, less interesting than what they do with it once they get it. Local management, after all, concerns more than a formulaic distribution of funds. According to England's education department: "Effective schemes of local management will enable governing bodies and headteachers to plan their use of resources—including their most valuable resource, their staff—to maximum effect in accordance with their own needs and priorities, and to make schools more responsive to their clients—parents, pupils, the local community and employers."[7]

The anecdotal evidence suggests this is indeed the case. Local management has allowed schools to tailor their discretionary resources to particular needs. Headteachers now have the freedom to move money between different budget headings; to spend more money on certain LEA services, such as in-service training, if they wish; to raise money; and to conserve where they can. All this has meant substantially more flexibility to spend money in ways that best suit individual schools and their communities.

Wherever we went, headteachers and deputies described the leeway they have under LMS they didn't have before. Significantly, many are targeting additional resources toward the classroom and toward students. Primary and secondary schools alike are spending more, as a percentage of the total school budget, on books, computer equipment, and materials than they did before local management was implemented in 1988, and less on running costs.[8] Many schools have hired teachers' aides. In Eastbourne, for instance, the principal of a primary school doubled the number of classroom assistants. Headteachers repeatedly pointed out the value of freeing teachers from other duties in order to *teach*.

Schools have also increased the nonteaching staff (with compensating reductions at the district level). At the Hinchingbrooke School in Cambridgeshire, the headteacher hired more secretaries to help teachers with such chores as photocopying. Support staff also assist headteachers and deputies with the increased administrative responsibilities that are part and parcel of local management.

Refurbishment of school property and redecoration have been one of the most noticeable benefits of local management. In Berkshire, a high school whitewashed dingy hallways and classrooms by putting aside $22,500 over four years. "That would have been difficult to do without LMS," the headteacher told us, because the authority had its own rolling maintenance program.

Schools are also saving money, particularly through conservation. Before LMS there was little incentive for schools to reduce the costs of heating, lighting, and other utilities. Now schools are more aware of wastage. In one London borough, a headteacher spotted a costly mistake with the telephone billing system. "We wouldn't have latched onto the problem had the bill gone straight to the LEA," he said. The potential for savings is small—estimated to be no more than 2 or 3 percent of a school's budget—but in large secondary schools, that amounts to about $45,000.[9]

Finally, local management has led schools to use their facilities in more creative, community-oriented ways. In Greenwich, a secondary school rents out rooms for local functions; the income helped pay for a communications satellite. Another school added to its coffers by providing car parking for the local racecourse.[10]

Overall, schools have taken well to managing their own finances, with more than 90 percent keeping expenditures within income.[11] Despite some grousing about the time it takes to prepare budgets, hire staff, order textbooks, oversee maintenance and utilities—to name just some of the new duties—few if any headteachers want to return to the days when the local authorities controlled their budgets. To help with the extra load, many schools have hired bursars or accountants to manage the finances.

After all, a typical secondary school has an annual budget of more than $2 million. In the beginning, most LEAs continued to manage and pay the bills; now, however, more and more schools keep their own accounts and checkbooks.

Perhaps as important as the state of the books is headteachers' state of mind. Financial independence has boosted morale.[12] Martin Roberts, head of the Cherwell secondary school in Oxford, said local management revitalized his job. "I was getting a bit bored by being a head in 1987," he explained. "But then LMS came in." He now has a $3 million budget at his disposal (before LMS, he had about $60,000 at his discretion). "With LMS, it's so much more efficient and you can do so much more—and you have to live with your decisions." In the first years of LMS, Cherwell built up a contingency fund of more than $200,000, extended the library, and put carpeting in every classroom to reduce noise. In years past, these improvements would have been possible only if they had been a priority of the LEA. "Once we got our money, we did it straightaway," said Roberts.

The benefits of local management, however, aren't universally appreciated. There is evidence to suggest a growing tension between headteachers and their management teams on the one hand and the classroom teachers on the other. The teams tend to take over the tasks of local management, oftentimes enlisting the help of a bursar or accountant; the teachers continue with the "real" work of the school.[13] Martin Roberts confessed to "an insubstantial crisis with the staff" over the management of Cherwell. "I spend a lot of time with the bursar on the financial side. I hope we haven't lost sight of educational priorities. What we have to say to the staff is, 'Look, everything has a cost.'" In many schools, financial problems, once handled outside the school building, are eclipsing educational ones—a problem exacerbated, of course, by per-capita funding and the pressure on each school to enroll as many students as possible.

Research by the Centre for Educational Studies at London's King's College confirms that local school management tends to drive a wedge between the classroom teachers and the market- and budget-oriented managers. "This gap is vividly present across our research on education reform," reports Stephen Ball, the research director.[14] One deputy headteacher explained that his job has shifted from "managing education to managing an educational institution." "[A]ll my non-teaching, non-contact time is taken up with going to meetings, or meeting people and organizing things, concerned with finance and resources, and not with promoting the grassroots educational program of the school."[15]

Headteachers who once concentrated solely on curricular and programmatic matters and who once took the time to teach an occasional class must now concentrate on ensuring his or her school's financial viability. The scramble for students, marketing, and outright fund-raising are time-consuming activities for many headteachers and deputies. As the government evidently intended, schools are forced to behave like small businesses in competition with one another. Still, most administrators recognize that they are leading an educational, not a commercial, enterprise. As schools grow more accustomed to the formidable tasks of local management, the conflicts between managers and teachers may subside.

Local management has altered more than the role of the headteacher. It has transformed dramatically the role of local authorities. By necessity, they have assumed a less directive approach, choosing instead to support schools, monitor their work, and assist with strategic planning. Those authorities led by resilient and entrepreneurial education directors are thriving. Others, however, are struggling to find a place in the new order.

While authorities have less control over spending levels and less budgetary control over individual schools than they once did, they retain powerful positions simply by overseeing schools in their districts, preparing development plans, handling personnel disputes, organizing in-service training and so forth. And they continue to employ staff in county schools, though governors increasingly assert their independence. Local authorities also continue to have a hand in the curriculum—by helping to implement the national curriculum rather than by imposing their own. Many keep an eye on districtwide skills, for instance, by measuring reading levels in the schools. They also assemble inspection teams that can bid for contracts under the rules established by the national Office of Standards in Education.

Schools, once the subsidiaries of the LEAs, are now consumers of their services. In Gloucestershire, the chief education officer has chosen to join the new education market rather than fight it. "We're more commercially oriented now. We're moving away from telling schools what to do," explained chief officer Keith Anderson. Instead, his authority decided to sell a variety of services, including payroll, personnel, maintenance, inspection, and consultancy services. Schools that have been delegated money to cover such expenses can choose to buy back the services they wish—or they can purchase them elsewhere. "Schools have the discretion to buy what they want when they want," explained Anderson. "This has been a useful rigor for us. We must ensure that our services are cost-effective." The authority reduced its full-time employees by 35 percent, or by 120 people. Most central offices are leaner than they once were; the administrative gain at the school level has been matched by a compensating loss at the district level.

In the inner London borough of Camden, the local education authority acts similarly. "The LEA influences rather than controls," said Peter Mitchell, the education director. School governors, he said, are pressuring headteachers to buy only core services from the local authority. "Many schools are taking their money and running. This places the LEA in a position of having to think through the management of its services."

Gloucestershire and Camden are pointing toward the LEA of the market-oriented future, but some fear that the commercial and consultative role will begin to eclipse the LEAs' vital social-welfare role. Who, if not local government, will ensure adequate school places, access for children with special needs, cooperation among schools, library services, and support for teachers? Who, if not local government, becomes responsible for strategic planning, for disseminating accurate information, and for monitoring quality? These important aspects of education can't be left entirely to individual schools, the marketplace, or the central government. They are particularly important for the primary schools, which have smaller and therefore less flexible budgets than secondaries. Without an LEA, many would have a hard time hiring peripatetic teachers (in music and art, for instance) or securing other services.

"People want LEAs to protect them," Tim Brighouse, Birmingham's chief education officer, said. Schools will retain their autonomy under local management, he predicted, but the local authorities must continue to act as "orchestrators and securers of fair play."

Camden's Peter Mitchell was more direct: "We need LEAs," he said, adding that otherwise the spectre is of an atomized system in which the authorities are left to rescue those students discarded by the schools—the disabled, disaffected, and undisciplined. "'Education otherwise,' we call it."

Even in Wandsworth, where just three of eleven secondary schools are maintained by the local authority, there is still a role for a central service provider. The chairman of the council's education committee, Elizabeth Howlett, says schools need LEAs. "There are bits they find frustrating and annoying, but other bits they find particularly supportive." She notes that Wandsworth transformed one closed school into a professional development center for teachers.

England's Association of Metropolitan Authorities, which represents the country's largest urban systems, argues that local authorities should regain some of the power lost under local management, including the right to intervene when schools aren't achieving the standards expected. "We need to find an appropriate balance between proper democratic accountability in delivering an important public service, and managerial freedom and flexibility which will release individual initiative and encourage the efficient use of resources," the association argues.[16]

There's little doubt that the historic role of the LEA—indeed, of any central administration—is a vital one. It has traditionally held together a planned and integrated system of education and balanced the tendency for each school to regard its own needs as paramount.[17] School autonomy and managerial flexibility are good things, but so are the safeguards provided by the local authorities.

While responsibility for the day-to-day operation of a school falls to headteachers and deputies, school management ultimately rests with the hundreds of thousands of individuals, many of them parents, who look after the country's schools. These are the governors, who've long had a part in English school life ("governors" and "managers" ran the schools long before the first elected school boards in the 1870s). For most of this century, however, their role was largely ceremonial. No longer. Governors today are like powerful corporate board members who work in concert with their chief executive officers, the headteachers. In effect, the governors picked up the pieces the LEAs were forced to leave behind after the passage of the Education Reform Act in 1988.

Governors began their rise to power in the early 1980s, as the consumerist movement and the rise of the "parentocracy" led to changes in the composition of the school boards. Elected parent governors joined the political nominees of the LEAs, teachers, the headteacher, and other community members (the size of the board depends on the size of the school). The advent of local management and financial delegation gave a further boost to governors' political profile and repositioned them at the center of school life.

Each state school, through its instruments and articles of government, establishes the rules and regulations by which governors must abide. By law, they must see that the national curriculum is implemented and tailor it to local needs; approve the budget; hire and fire staff (in consultation with the LEA, in the case of headteachers and other senior staff); award pay supplements; set disciplinary policy; provide information about the school to parents; hear complaints; and prepare annual reports.

Although the responsibility for school management is relatively new, most (60 percent) exhibit the hallmarks of good practice.[18] Governing styles, however, vary tremendously from school to school, with some governing bodies micromanaging and others surrendering almost all control to senior staff. It's not surprising that the most vibrant and effective schools we visited had strong, though not domineering, governing bodies that worked cooperatively with the headteachers. Cherwell's headteacher Martin Roberts said: "I've got to negotiate policy with the governors—or with governors and staff simultaneously. I've got to make sure that all elements of the constituency move along simultaneously."

The principal of the Garth Hill School in Berkshire explained the new partnership between her administration and the nineteen governors on the secondary school's board this way: "The major implication since 1988 has been working with the governors. Now their powers are so diverse. They can't govern by remote control anymore. . . . They can dismiss staff, so it's important to get a rapport going, to set up linkages between the governors and the school's department heads. This takes a lot of time for senior management."

It also takes a lot of time for the governors, who are, after all, volunteers. The former director of the Institute for Education at the University of London told us he had to stand down as a school governor. He was only half joking when he said serving on the board of his neighborhood school was more demanding than directing England's largest and most prestigious teacher-training institute. The job, especially for the chairmen and committee leaders, can be taxing. Training courses, offered by the LEAs, universities, and the National Association of Governors and Managers, help familiarize governors with school finance, accounting, education law, and other aspects of school management. In many schools, however, there are insufficient candidates for board membership, and there are often vacancies. In the poorest urban neighborhoods and in small villages, recruitment can be especially difficult. Disadvantaged social groups are underrepresented.[19] Single parents don't have the time or the will to serve. The problem led the London borough of Southwark, one of the city's toughest and poorest neighborhoods, to organize a commission to encourage more members of the community to serve.

Still, governors' power over school administration and personnel is mightily apparent, as a celebrated case in Hackney, London's inner city, illustrates. In 1993, the head of a primary school found herself in the media spotlight after refusing free tickets for some of the schoolchildren to attend the ballet *Romeo and Juliet*. According to accounts, she objected to the blatantly "heterosexual" storyline. The borough's chief education officer, reacting to adverse publicity about the headteacher's political and sexual orientation, called for her suspension, but the governors and parents stood by her, pointing to the fact that she had helped raise achievement and improve school discipline. The local authority, the nominal employer, found itself stymied by the school's own loyal constituency.

It's no wonder that governing bodies have been described as the "sleeping giant" of the education reforms. When they band together, governors are a formidable new bloc in the national politics of education. In the spring of 1995, for example, governors and parents throughout the country raised their voices in protest over the central government's refusal to fund the teachers' pay rise. In some local authorities, governors threatened to quit unless more money was made available for staffing. In Derbyshire, eighteen secondary school governors did resign rather than fire teachers and cut $375,000 from the school's 1995-96 budget. The local authority was forced to take over the school.

The incident in Hackney and the nationwide revolt demonstrate the angry face of the parentocracy the Conservatives helped to create. They also exemplify some of the problems raised by the empowerment of governors. Lines of authority aren't as straight as they once were. Prior to the government's reforms, a local authority would have assumed responsibility for a headteacher's actions. Today, however, the chain of command is likely to break down, as it did in Hackney, if parents, governors, and chief education officers clash. Before 1988, parents and governors would have blamed their local authority for a budget squeeze, larger classes, and insufficient staffing; today, though, local management has made them more knowledgeable about funding sources and school finance; it's also made them more politically savvy. They know that school funding depends primarily on grants from the central government.

The recent conflicts between governors and others who manage education, whether county officials or government ministers, suggest the need to clarify the rules and regulations pertaining to personnel and other aspects of school administration. As Birmingham's chief education officer points out, "Nobody thought a governing body wouldn't behave sensibly." Fortunately, most do. When they don't, however, the course of action isn't always clear.

Most people in England today concur that local management is a sensible approach to decision making, but there is also concern that devolution has forced education to become "too parochial," as Gloucestershire's chief education officer put it. "The community is wider than the school," he said. And it must be said that the country is wider than the community. Who wins when the central government seeks to hold down spending while the local authority seeks to keep schools open and class sizes small? This is just one of the financial and political dilemmas raised by the coexistence of central control and local management.

Local management can't work miracles. According to veteran education writer Stuart Maclure, there's been a temptation to overstate the amount of autonomy that the 1988 Education Reform Act promised. Financial delegation, he points out, takes place within fairly tight monetary and educational constraints.[20] Nor is it a cure for underachievement, bad teaching, or managerial ineptitude. Its success depends entirely on the abilities of the headteachers and the governors—no small order.

But greater managerial freedom at the school site is undoubtedly a benefit. LMS has been a lever for some important changes, both within the schools themselves and between schools and their local authorities. While it's too soon to say whether the strategy directly affects the quality of teaching or pupil achievement,[21] it can lead to improvements in the classroom. It has led also to improvements in the attitudes of headteachers, who express a renewed sense of professional fulfillment. While there are challenges, complications and, in a minority of cases, some questionable practices, the early years of local management in England suggest that schools can take their money and run in promising directions.

Grant-maintained Schools

Local management offers schools a good measure of financial independence within the established structures of local government. Grant-maintained schools, on the other hand, derive their independence by existing *outside* that structure. "GM" schools are owned, as well as managed, by their governing bodies. Buildings and grounds pass from the local authority to the governors, who also employ personnel and assume responsibility for recruitment, training, suspension, and dismissal. They must decide whether to adhere to previously determined salary agreements or whether to negotiate new contracts. They must provide school meals and maintain the physical plant (though the education authority continues to provide certain pupil-related services, such as transportation). They coordinate admissions policies, and they can invest money and acquire property.

But if the step from local management to grant-maintained status appears small on paper, it is a giant ideological leap. By distributing funds directly to schools, rather than through the local authorities, the government sought to create a set of competing institutions that would challenge the policies and practices of the locally maintained schools. In fact, the Conservatives hoped that grant-maintained schools would bust the local schools' "monopoly."

It's little wonder that the campaign to create grant-maintained schools polarized the education service in England. Tensions continue today. As Conservative ministers urge all schools to opt out, the local authorities defend their right to remain the principal providers of state education. This tug of war, rife with misinformation and propaganda on both sides, pits "St. Lea" against "monstrous GMs," as one principal put it.[22] Birmingham's chief education officer, Tim Brighouse, says simply: "GM is really a political correctness issue."

Any state school can choose to opt out, using a process painstakingly crafted by lawmakers and set out in the Education Reform Act of 1988. The procedure hinges on a parental ballot. The governing body can pass a resolution to hold an election, or a group of parents representing 20 percent of the student body can petition the governors. Under a law passed in 1993, each governing body must consider annually whether to hold a ballot.

Parents whose children are registered at the school receive ballots and explanatory information in the mail within ten weeks of the governors' resolution or parents' petition. The local electoral commission administers the distribution of ballots and the vote count. Pamphlets published by the local authorities or other interest groups must be circulated separately. Usually schools hold public meetings to discuss the implications of opting out. The law makes no special provision for teachers, though opting out may well change the terms and conditions of their employment.

The ballots ask parents whether the governing body should apply formally for grant-maintained status. The vote is a simple *yes* or *no*. If fewer than 50 percent of eligible parents choose to vote or if the result is a tie, then a second ballot must be held within fourteen days. That result is decisive, no matter how many parents choose to exercise their right. A simple majority rules.

If the vote is favorable, the governing body has several months to prepare and publish statutory proposals, including the school's articles of government and its aims, and submit them to the secretary of state, who rules on the merits of the case. The LEA, or any other group, is permitted to state its objections.

Today, there are about one thousand grant-maintained schools, most of them in the secondary sector. While the number is a small fraction of the twenty-four thousand schools in England and Wales, they represent a quarter of all secondary schools and educate more than six hundred thousand pupils.

Why do schools opt out? Most apply for grant-maintained status because they seek independence from their local authority. According to a 1994 survey of more than five hundred grant-maintained schools, 90 percent said they opted out for increased autonomy.[23] "The freedom to decide our own priorities and to act upon them speedily, has released energy, enterprise and commitment in a way impossible to conceive of when we were local-authority controlled," responded one headteacher.

But the reasons for opting out are more complicated than the respondents' answers might suggest. A variety of factors prompts schools to consider GM status. In the early years, a large proportion of schools opted out because they were slated to close. The process was often initiated by headteachers who were anxious about the future of their institutions, rather than by groups of parents or governors.[24] In such cases, the government found that, on the one hand, declining enrollments led it to demand school consolidation and closure; on the other hand, a zealous commitment to self-governing schools led it to rescue some schools that should have been closed for purposes of sound planning and economic efficiency.

Opting out is also a kind of protest vote. Many schools refuse to put up with bureaucratic ineptitude and political interference. The Small Heath School in Birmingham was among the first secondaries to opt out—despite vocal opposition and protracted legal challenge. According to Cecil Knight, the headteacher, grant-maintained status offered the school a chance to fight for the life of the children caught in a downward spiral of neglect: "What price educational opportunities when your pupils are being denied adequate teaching, books and equipment and being put at risk by falling plaster, penetrating rainwater and soggy wiring? Insofar as we knew that times were hard we sympathized with our LEA, but we felt that funds were being allocated according to mistaken priorities. Frankly we were tired of listening to the ceaseless litanies of 'It can't be done' and 'Don't blame us, blame the government' from politicians and occasionally from officers. Here at last was a golden opportunity for us to set our own priorities and to create our own budget without depriving others."[25]

In Wandsworth, many of the secondary schools reacted against a proposed magnet program that would have changed their character. Principals feared the introduction of pupil selection and early specialization. The Burntwood School, which we describe in more detail later, was among those resisting a makeover. The governors voted to seek grant-maintained status, and 80 percent of the parents approved.

Disaffection from local government and the quest for self-determination are more common in some districts than others, however. Thus, GM schools appear in geographic clusters. In 1994, 64 percent of all grant-maintained schools were in 15 of the 117 local education authorities in England and Wales. Thirty-three authorities had no grant-maintained schools at all, and two dozen others had very few.[26]

Finally, schools opt out for the financial rewards offered by a government eager to see these schools proliferate and prosper. In theory, grant-maintained schools were to be treated no better or worse than other schools maintained by the state. But in fact they are the beneficiaries of preferential funding. Grant-maintained schools receive an annual maintenance grant, derived by using the LEA's own formula for funding its schools, *plus funds for central services once provided by that authority.* In general, this amounts to a 15-percent credit. These calculations, while intended to hold harmless the local authorities, in fact favor grant-maintained schools.

In addition to the maintenance grant, GM schools receive special grants designed to help these "new" institutions function independently. Transitional grants offset the start-up costs associated with incorporation, including extra staff and computer systems for administration. There are other special grants for staff development and training of governors. Capital grants help GM schools renovate or expand. A school that opts out can expect a bonus of $150,000 or more. Burntwood received more than a million dollars for new science facilities and other capital improvements. While it's true that grant-maintained schools must meet the increased costs of services once provided by the LEA (it can cost more for an individual school to purchase goods and services than an LEA), the grants have proved generous. The government's chief inspector reports: "There is no doubt that from the outset grant-maintained schools have greatly benefited financially from their change of status."[27]

Whatever the reasons schools opt out, few if any want to opt back in. Headteachers and governors relish self-government. Brigid Beattie, principal of Burntwood, is among the GM converts. "I don't believe in local education authorities," she told us. Freedom from the local district has led her to be more innovative and to use monies more wisely, she said. She and the twenty-four-member governing board are responsible for a budget of $4.75 million and the education of thirteen hundred girls ages eleven to eighteen, most of them ethnic minorities.

The school appears to manage well without the support of local government. Beattie, a dedicated educator and able administrator, has delegated considerable responsibilities to others. "We did not have sufficient expertise on the governing body, in the school office or among the senior team to be confident that we could handle the major areas of finance, personnel and administration that we were taking over from the LEA," she explains. "We decided, as a deputy head was retiring, to use this post to finance the appointment of a director of finance and administration." Burntwood chose not to buy back the LEA's "schoolkeeping" services, which Beattie described as costly and inefficient. Instead, the school hired a site manager to be responsible for the upkeep of the building and grounds.

Beattie described the first years of GM status as exhilarating ones. "It has revealed the LEA as an emperor without clothes—it was hard to remember the value of any of its services. The most liberating factor about GM status is how quickly minor changes—but changes that enhance the working conditions of both staff and students—can be effected."[28] The school increased staff salaries, successfully bid for more funds for disadvantaged students, spent more on the curriculum, and improved the cleaning and catering services.

Burntwood is a GM success story, and there are scores of others. But other GM schools hint at the dilemmas raised by the strategy. Unlike Burntwood, which opted out in order to remain a girls' comprehensive, some schools opt out to remain selective. In certain areas of the country, the old grammar schools make up a disproportionate number of the GM total. In Kent, for example, where a tradition of academic selection at age eleven continues, almost half of the county's secondary schools opted out. This isn't entirely surprising; the strategy was intended to help save some of the country's remaining selective schools, most of which were converted into comprehensives between the late 1960s and 1980s.

More troubling, though, is that many GM schools, by establishing their own admissions procedures and policies on exclusion and expulsion, are *becoming* selective institutions, raising fears that the policy threatens equal access. Originally, grant-maintained schools were barred from changing their "character"—including their admissions policies; government guidelines recommended a five-year moratorium on any revisions. But a 1993 education act eased the restrictions. The Department for Education already has allowed a handful of schools to select up to 50 percent of their intake. Still others have been accused of "selection by stealth." A study of the first one hundred grant-maintained schools found that 30 percent of the GM schools that called themselves "comprehensive" were using school reports, parental and pupil interviews, or examinations to select students.[29]

This is a predictable result when there are more applicants than school spaces. A choice must be made. Many GM schools consider the family's proximity to the school or give preference to siblings, just as most LEAs do when assigning students. But the research suggests that some GM schools are resorting to more subjective techniques. The reason isn't hard to fathom. When money follows the child, schools avoid incurring extra expenses—and trouble. Students with behavioral problems or learning disabilities are more expensive to educate and are oftentimes more difficult. A spokesman for the Grant-Maintained Schools Centre, which aids GM schools and promotes the policy, admitted that headteachers and governors may be "thinking uncomfortable thoughts—like wouldn't it be nice to exclude this pupil. . . ."

In fact, GM schools, unlike LEA schools, can expel pupils whose behavior does not match expectations. This is precisely what's happening in Kent. GM schools are picking and choosing pupils and refusing to take students excluded from other schools, according to the county's education director, Roy Pryke. "This is leading to a real fear among non-GM schools that they will become 'sink schools.' We now have schools choosing pupils instead of parents having more choices," he explained.[30] In the historic town of Canterbury, all but one secondary has become a grant-maintained school. When boys with disciplinary problems were expelled from the GM schools, the local authority was obliged to find spaces for them. "Where in the end do you put the children?" Pryke asked. "Are we going to establish schools for the rejects? Produce concentrations of rejected children?" Similarly, in southwest Hertfordshire, where most schools are grant-maintained, students scramble for placement. "That's a mess—not knowing where the kids are going to be," commented Marianne Coleman, whose research for Leicester University has highlighted some of the risks of GM policy. The rise in exclusions and expulsions is one of the most significant—and disturbing—changes since the advent of grant-maintained schools.

In other ways, GM schools seem to "appeal to snobbishness," as one educator put it. Researchers from Warwick University observed that many GM schools possess a "reinvigorated traditionalism."[31] For example, there's a tendency among GM schools to introduce uniforms, dress codes, and strict discipline. One even favored fountain pens over ballpoints. It would seem that some GM schools are making themselves over in the image of the elitist grammar schools, as Conservative policymakers had hoped. In fact, anecdotal evidence suggests that certain parents, teachers, and other community members have come to think of GM schools as somehow superior to schools controlled by the local authorities. Thus, grant-maintained schools threaten to recreate the academic hierarchy that the comprehensive movement all but dismantled. One headteacher told us that his own conversations with prospective parents revealed a subtle preference for GM schools—a trend he called "really aggravating" but nevertheless instrumental in his own school's decision to opt out. His administrative deputies shared this perception. "'We'll be second-class,' they said. They said it cynically, but there's a degree of truth to it." Parents may perceive GM schools as adding diversity, but too often it is a diversity without a difference.

Perhaps the biggest dilemma is that GM schools and local schools operate on uneven playing fields. The years of financial favoritism to GM schools have boosted one sector at the expense of the other and fractured the education service. "In the abstract, the system is immoral," one headteacher told us. "It is skewed financially and otherwise. I wouldn't have had anything to do with it. I still think it stinks." But this head of a Catholic boys' school in the London borough of Barnet was faced with a "crisis of conscience." In the end, he yielded to pressure from his staff and governors. The high school became grant-maintained because the extra money was a boon. "I'm paid to look after the welfare of my students and this school," he confessed. "If we're talking about surviving in the marketplace, it doesn't matter how long any extra money may last. It's survival of the fittest. I'm not very proud of that as a deep educational thinker. But I don't want my life to end in tatters running a failing school."

As in many jurisdictions around the country, Barnet was faced with the GM "domino effect." First one secondary opted out, then another, then another. When this happens, the local authorities become increasingly cash poor, and the local schools suffer. The LEAs can't provide a consistent level of services. As one headteacher in Lincolnshire put it: "The local authority might say that it can provide the same level of services but it is questionable. The anxiety is that you will be left behind as the runt."[32]

In Kent, where half the county's 126 secondary schools opted out, the trend has caused havoc with the finances of the local authority, reducing the amount of money for schools that remain under local control and diminishing the authority's capacity to support them. When a large primary school opts out, it takes with it the money needed to finance one nursery school class, according to education director Pryke. "Is the development of the GM sector going to contribute more to raising standards than the extension of nursery education?" he asks.[33]

Of course, schools that must vie for students and funds don't necessarily care how opting out affects neighboring schools or their local authority. "Survival of the fittest" is indeed the operative theme. As the head of a Berkshire secondary told us: "I wouldn't want to do it (apply for GM status). But if it's best for the school, I'll push for it." Says Roy Pryke: "Schools find themselves in an invidious position—caught between a narrow self-interest in resources and broader concerns about the community at large."[34]

Finally, there are those who question both the independence of grant-maintained schools and their accountability to democratic institutions. While many GM heads elatedly describe their liberation from local bureaucracy, critics contend that the vaunted autonomy is a fiction. GM schools, they say, have simply "opted into" state control, exchanging the rules and regulations of the local authority for the rules and regulations of the central government. The Department for Education has always kept close watch on the schools' use of public money. Now, even tighter bureaucratic control is inevitable, since the Funding Agency for Schools, created by an act of Parliament in 1993, has begun to determine GM budgets and monitor GM policy and planning. The agency is expected to work alongside the local authorities to provide sufficient school spaces wherever there is a concentration of GM schools.

But who will be the final arbiter? The local authorities who answer to elected representatives, the political appointees of the Funding Agency for Schools, or the secretary of education? The question of accountability for GM schools is not a minor one. Unelected members make up the majority on GM governing boards. According to Kent's Roy Pryke: "The push from the Department for Education for schools to opt out seems . . . to have little or nothing to do with improving education and has everything to do with the emasculation of locally accountable influence in favor of centralization of power."[35]

Grant-maintained schools were devised to expand choice and raise academic standards. Have they? Our own observations suggest they have yet to extend significantly the options available to parents. They have not added to the existing stock or increased the variety. Like all other state schools, they must deliver the national curriculum. Parents tend to choose grant-maintained schools for the same reasons they would choose any school—because of its proximity to home, its academic reputation, and its ethos. Many aren't even aware of the school's governing structure, nor do parents report a greater sense of control in the running of GM schools.[36] Self-governing schools have yet to capture parents' imaginations.[37] As of the spring of 1994, 20 percent of ballots were initiated by parents.[38] In this sense, the GM "market" has developed in ways other than those envisaged by Conservative policymakers and such American advocates as John E. Chubb and Terry M. Moe, authors of *Politics, Markets, and America's Schools,* who praised opting out as a "truly revolutionary idea."[39] Parents, the putative beneficiaries of the law, aren't applying it.

In fact, a persuasive case can be made that grant-maintained schools actually diminish parental choice and educational innovation. Many schools have used the legislation to preserve their status or to prevent changes that might have been in the best interest of the community at large. In the case of selective schools, the choice is more often the schools' than the parents'. Where there are large concentrations of grant-maintained schools, the local authorities are struggling to secure an equitable geographical distribution of school places, leaving little or no choice for students not accepted to GM schools.

As for academic standards, it's difficult to make before-and-after comparisons. Today's grant-maintained school is yesterday's locally maintained school. In September 1993, the government's chief inspector reported that the "standards achieved and the quality of learning were on average better in the self-governing schools than in LEA-maintained schools." But, as the chief inspector notes, a high proportion of GM schools are selective (13.5 percent at the time of the inspectors' report, compared with only 4.5 percent nationally).[40] And most—though by no means all—of the GM schools are in suburban and rural areas and significantly less affected by the social and economic disadvantages that tend to depress student achievement in urban schools. Still, the promising performance in the GM sector bears watching—whether it's the result of more money or greater autonomy or both.

Grant-maintained schools, like many schools thriving under local management, have been improved. Headteachers and governors have used their money to increase teaching and support staff and to refurbish buildings—tangible benefits of self-governance. GM schools often exude high morale and a sense of pride. While these attributes may not contribute directly to greater choice or to higher achievement, they are important to the school community, adding life and energy to the enterprise.

Why, then, aren't more schools opting out? Some GM partisans maintain that self-governing schools were, until recently, politically vulnerable institutions; before 1995, the Labor Party pledged to abolish them. Labor's current leaders, however, say they are willing to accept grant-maintained schools if funding is equitable and if they cooperate more fully with local education authorities in some areas, such as special education.

School administrators have also been wary about the financial benefits of opting out, knowing that the government's largess to the GM sector cannot last. In 1993, the government revised the funding regulations in jurisdictions where grant-maintained schools serve 10 percent or more of the student population. In such places, a common funding formula has replaced calculations based on the local authorities' variable budgets. Just how this formula will affect the finances of grant-maintained schools remains unclear, but the rules are expected to blunt the financial advantages of opting out. According to the Local Schools Information, an advocacy group representing the local authorities, the central government's direct control of GM spending could result in smaller subsidies than headteachers, governors, and parents have been led to expect.

Political uncertainty and budgetary confusion, then, could explain why the number of ballots peaked in October 1992. Since then fewer and fewer parents have voted "yes" to opting out.

But there is another explanation for the declining interest. There's not a lot GM status can do for a school that local management, a far less divisive governance and administrative strategy, cannot. Schools enjoy substantial financial autonomy now that districts must delegate at least 85 percent of the school budget. But they also derive satisfaction, and some essential services, by continuing to affiliate with the local authority. We spoke with many headteachers who want to collaborate, for reasons both practical and philosophical, with local government. As Geoff Turner, a deputy headteacher, put it: "I know there are inherent weaknesses in working with the local education authority, we all moan about it, but I for one feel part of a national educational system; I believe in collaboration, and I believe in equal access for all."[41] For some schools, in some circumstances, opting out might be the best course. But for most schools, LEAs continue to offer a safety net and a vital link to the community.

City Technology Colleges

City technology colleges are a special case. These fifteen secondary schools represent the government's first attempt to build schools outside LEA boundaries. Like grant-maintained schools, CTCs are owned and managed by their governing bodies. Unlike them, however, they quite literally bank on their association with business and industry. Since 1987, some two hundred corporate sponsors have contributed more than $55 million, mostly in construction and capital costs, to the handful of city technology colleges dotted around England. In exchange, the sponsors help govern the schools, which cater to youngsters age eleven to eighteen.

By mixing private enterprise and public schooling, the British government hoped to "cement the permanence of the link between education and the world of employment."[42] By building brand-new schools dedicated to the practical applications of mathematics, science, and computer programming, the government hoped to promote an "educational culture" that is technologically, vocationally, and internationally oriented. In short, CTCs offer a new scholastic prototype.

CTCs have become managerial and curricular testbeds—after all, they don't have to abide by the rules and regulations of the LEAs or the teaching unions. For instance, they have imposed a longer school day, and some have adopted a longer school year. The typical CTC pupil spends thirty-one hours in class and extracurricular activities per week, compared with twenty-three hours for students in other state schools. Several CTCs have extended the school year from 190 days to 200 days, dividing it into five eight-week terms, with two-week breaks in between. CTCs were forced to make a virtue out of necessity. The schools could not fulfill all the requirements of the national curriculum *and* spend extra time on math, science, and technology unless they added to students' and teachers' schedules.

Many CTCs begin early in the morning and continue until well into the evening. The Performing Arts and Technology School in outer London, open from 7:30 A.M. until 9 P.M., has trouble keeping the youngsters away. "We had to make a rule that students under sixteen left by 7 P.M.—and then we heard complaints that the under-sixteens were unfairly discriminated against!" says principal Anne Rumney.

CTC students are generally enthusiastic about the longer day, as are working parents and employers, who find that CTC schedules mesh better with their own. Teachers, by and large, are also committed to the longer days, though many report fatigue. They are expected to work from 8:30 A.M. to 5 P.M., a schedule that includes teaching, tutoring, and supervising work experience and extracurricular activities. The 1,265 hours stipulated in the Teachers' Pay and Conditions Act has little relevance for those who choose to work in CTCs. According to one survey, "staff say they knew what they were taking on before they were hired. They feel that there is no comparison with the state sector. Everyone puts in the hours, and the job satisfaction is enormous."[43]

The use of time is not the only difference between CTCs and conventional high schools. The use of space can be novel, too. With their sleek reception areas and computer banks, these purpose-built institutions bear more resemblance to modern corporate offices than to schools. The organization and design help to convey the schools' mission to train young people for work. In fact, students are encouraged to think like "employees" as they mimic workday routines. At Thomas Telford in Shropshire, for instance, youngsters dress formally, as if for the office (many do serve as interns off campus). At Brooke Weston, in the British

Midlands, pupils register in the morning using electronically controlled "smart cards." The workplace analogy extends to school administration. At ADT College in the London borough of Wandsworth, the management structure reflects that of industry. The school is led by a chief executive, a managing director in charge of curriculum, and a board of academic and administrative directors.

Industrial ties trickle down through the curriculum. Dixons CTC, named after a leading electronics retailer, pays close attention to electronic engineering and educational technology. The Performing Arts and Technology School, built with money from the British Record Industry Trust, borrows its curricular themes from the entertainment industry. The school has impressively equipped TV and radio studios, dance halls, set-design workshops, and composing rooms. In the school's main lobby, there's a student-run box office that sells discount tickets for London's shows. There's even a "retail unit," or school store, where students learn marketing skills.

Increasingly, CTCs are pushing and pulling at the framework of the national curriculum by developing courses best suited to their students' interests. Cross-disciplinary departments are common. The ADT College has an "Enterprise and World Resources Directorate" that includes geography, mathematics, information technology, history, business education, and religious studies. Djanogly in Nottingham has a combined program of business studies, information technology, and modern languages, including Spanish, German, French and Russian. The CTC has links with similar schools in Europe.

CTCs are also pioneering new pathways for students, especially for those sixteen and over. Unlike American students, who earn a general diploma for the successful completion of high school, English students must strive for certificates awarded by an array of examinations boards. Typically, pupils must choose between the so-called "A-level" coursework in traditional academic subjects or concentrate on achieving a vocational qualification. CTCs, however, are encouraging their students to strive for both academic and vocational qualifications. A student who wrote an essay on the operation of a sound studio, for instance, might qualify for an A-level certificate in English and a vocational award. In this way, CTCs are beginning to bridge the divide between the academic and vocational.

CTCs are immensely popular with students. Each year, these special schools receive far more applicants than they can accommodate. Attendance rates exceed the national average. Who gets in? By law, CTCs must serve children of different abilities, and student bodies must reflect the composition of the mostly urban catchment areas in which the schools are situated. But achieving a broadly representative sample isn't easy. Entry, after all, depends partly on self-selection (the motivation of prospective pupils to submit an application) and selection (almost all CTCs conduct interviews or require examinations). Most CTCs try to be comprehensive; Kingshurst, for instance, ensures a range of students by dividing candidates into nine academic and social groups. Still, studies have found that CTCs cater to students with particular abilities and interests and that they are, therefore, essentially selective institutions designed for, as one critic put it, a "deserving" segment of the school population. Those most in need—the disaffected inner-city youths at risk of academic failure—aren't benefiting.[44]

But those who do choose CTCs—and those who are chosen by them—are pleased with the education they receive. The CTCs we visited buzzed with energy and enthusiasm. The facilities were clean and well-stocked. Students and staff seemed to share a missionary zeal. Torsten Friedag, vice principal of the performing arts school, says: "Most students want to be here. I now believe all schools can be like this. It has something to do with money and resources, but the staff need to believe in the school's mission. If a school is able to provide a broad education but specialize in something, then it has created an environment people are happy to be in." Indeed, the happiness of Marcus Horner and Kizzy Perkins, two arts students who showed us around the school, was palpable. Horner, while pursuing an interest in English literature and drama, was also acting, composing, and organizing gigs for bands. Perkins, who "loves the arts side of things," was learning the marketing skills related to the music industry.

New facilities, curricular innovations, administrative autonomy, corporate backing, and eager students don't necessarily guarantee instant success, however. One has only to travel to London's East End and to

Bacon's CTC to understand that these pathbreaking secondary schools encounter the same challenges as other urban schools in deprived areas. The $30 million building, completed in 1991 with the help of the Southwark Diocesan Board of Education, the London Docklands Development Corporation, and a charitable foundation, replaced the original Bacon's Church of England school founded in the neighborhood in 1703. The old Victorian school building had fallen on hard times; so had its students and faculty. There were high rates of expulsion, poor exam results, behavioral problems among the students, frequent turnover among the staff. Teachers were in short supply.

The new CTC was an attempt to "resurrect"—principal Peter Jenkins' word—a dying school. Students and staff were expected to shed the weight of collective failure and begin anew. According to accounts, the first years were chaotic. The building itself was incomplete; architects and subcontractors went bust; rooms weren't ready; there was no playground. "I thought I was going to come into a situation where the building and the equipment were perfect but the students were difficult. In fact, it was the other way round," says Jenkins.

More than four years later, this school cum community center (there are impressive sports and leisure facilities, including a pub) struggles to prove itself. The school is divided into color-coded "houses," and youngsters move up with a tutor group. About a third of the students arrive with severe reading disabilities, and the chronically low achievement that characterized the old Bacon's has yet to disappear. But there are signs of hope. Exam results are improving, if only incrementally, and a handful of pupils have gone on to college and university—unprecedented for a school notorious in recent times for alienating students rather than aiding them.

"There's tremendous pressure for flash results," says Jenkins. "It's like being under a microscope." The central government, which has invested so much in the CTC initiative, scrutinizes the performance indicators not only at Bacon's but at all fifteen schools. So far, results have been mixed. Achievement, as measured by scores on the school-leaving examinations taken at sixteen, was below the national average at a third of the colleges, including Bacon's and the performing arts school, in 1994.[45] Jenkins warns that schools that admit some of the most vulnerable members of society can't improve according to government timetables.

We would add that test scores aren't the only measure of success. CTCs seem to be working in other ways. Students, as well as faculty, are committed to their institutions. There is a community spirit and a manifest pride. To be sure, plenty of locally maintained schools exhibit these characteristics as well, but we observed that CTCs seem especially vital, whether due to the institutions' newness, their singular mission, their selectivity, their autonomy, or the links to business and commerce.

On this last point, we note that while CTCs certainly point to the potential of the alliance between education and industry, they also demonstrate the inherent limitations of that alliance. The project was initiated in the belief that the corporate community was as keen to aid urban education and extend parents' range of choices as the government. But the original scheme to build twenty schools outside the jurisdiction of the local education authorities concerned not only the teachers and district administrators but many CEOs and other business representatives as well. Financial sponsorship did not come as readily, nor was it as generous, as Conservative policymakers had hoped. The government, through the City Technology College Trust, spent a lot of energy cajoling those in the private sector to become patrons.

In the end, fund-raising did not match expectations. The government spent 80 percent of the total cost of construction. The high capital expenditure (about $200 million) forced an end to the program in 1993, when the last CTC opened in Bristol. There simply wasn't enough corporate interest or revenue to sustain it.

"CTCs were never meant to be ends in themselves," explains Clive Andrews, of the City Technology College Trust. "They were always meant to be exemplars. They have created greater choice in certain geographical areas. They have led to technology development. And the knock-on effect has created a considerable amount of choice."

Andrews is referring to the fact that other locally maintained and grant-maintained schools are beginning to affiliate with corporate sponsors and local business to become "technology colleges." So far, about fifty secondaries have raised at least $150,000 in private funding (matched by the Department for Education) to help finance new computer networks and laboratories. Sponsors are expected to become an integral part of the school, providing work experience for students and influencing the direction and management of the school by taking up a seat on the governing body.

Still, we have our doubts about whether sufficient private sponsors will be found to help the majority of schools in England. Some schools will undoubtedly benefit from their association with business and industry. Others won't be so lucky. Hence, the strategy runs the risk of leading to further inequality. This is precisely the objection many have to CTCs. Like grant-maintained schools, they receive preferential treatment. While the government calculates running costs by using the same per-capita funding formula that applies to all state schools (the total amounted to $75 million in 1994), the CTCs receive lavish private gifts and donations. The Performing Arts and Technology School gets an annual stipend of $75,000 from the British Record Industry Trust for new equipment and computer software, for instance. Sponsors such as this add tremendously to a school's financial and cultural capital.

But what about other schools? More to the point, perhaps, what about private patrons' ability to support CTCs and technology colleges in future? What happens if local businesses pull out because they can no longer afford the price of sponsorship? What then? Can the central government pick up the costs of maintaining the expensive hardware that helps to keep these schools on the technological edge? The CTC initiative suggests that private sponsors can be valuable helpmates. But they do not seek to build schools or to become full-fledged partners in the business of education.

WHAT ARE WE TO MAKE of these variations on the theme of autonomy? Could schools in the United States go it alone? Should they?

The success of local management in England suggests that school districts here at home would do well to look at devolution. As it is now, too many are caught between the demands of the statehouse and those of the schoolhouse. State legislators want to see higher standards, more accountable schools, better results. Principals and teachers want to exert greater control within their schools.

What if districts were to assume a more strategic role, as LEAs have in England? As Ernest Boyer points out in the foreword to this report, district-level administrators could retain key positions as basic service providers, monitors of educational quality, disseminators of information, and strategic planners, while delegating more money and more managerial authority to the principals, teachers, and parents within the schools. Some districts, following the example of Chicago and Kentucky, might choose to elect school councils. But financial delegation and managerial autonomy do not depend on new layers of government or lay representation. School boards, democratically elected bodies with a noble history, are well situated to cast themselves in a new role.

We're convinced that schools will become more responsive to their students, to parents, and to the neighborhood if they're given more latitude to do what they want when they want. Principals will become more engaged, and students will benefit from the greater attention paid to the physical plant, to classroom resources, and to the deployment of teachers, aides, and staff. The English example suggests that local management can strengthen the community within the school. Schools, once satellites orbiting around a central office, are now exhibiting some self-determination.

Of course, the adoption of local management along English lines raises crucial questions. For instance: How would the money be distributed to individual schools, by what calculation? A hard-hearted per-capita formula, like the one favored by England's Conservative government, can lead to stark divisions between rich and poor. In the end, districts would have to develop their own schemes, keeping close attention to the socioeconomic profile of the community, the size of the school, maintenance costs, salary schedules, the local cost of living, and other factors.

How would school-based management affect teachers and their unions? Who would train principals to prepare budgets? By what means would school managers—the principals and/or council members—be held accountable for their actions? These and many other questions would have to be answered carefully. But, based on the evidence from England, we think longstanding relationships among teachers, principals, superintendents, and school boards can change, that bureaucracies can shrink and that hierarchies can shift without the collapse of the governing superstructure that has served schools fairly well. Indeed, we think that local management could buttress that structure.

Finally, a word on charter schools, which are gaining popularity in many states. Are these new schools the grant-maintained schools in America's future? A very different scholastic tradition and a unique set of political pressures led to the creation of grant-maintained schools. And different rules apply: in England, parents vote to opt out from their local authority, whereas founders of charters are bound by a contract, usually with the local governing body. Still, there are obvious parallels. States are turning to charter schools for much the same reasons that the British government turned to grant-maintained schools: to broaden choice within the public domain and to test the value of self-governance. The questions that hang over the English grant-maintained schools today will hang over American charter schools as well. Can these schools balance the twin and often competing demands for autonomy and accountability? Will they fracture the system? Will they threaten equal opportunity? Participants in the growing movement for charter schools will find these questions unavoidable.

CHAPTER III

Choice: Going to Market

LOCAL MANAGEMENT, GRANT-MAINTAINED SCHOOLS, and even the handful of city technology colleges are all part of a larger strategy to promote choice and a more competitive market in British education. Devolution of control and diversity of provision were crucial, policymakers reasoned, if schools were to become more responsive to parental preferences, more accountable to their governing bodies, and more efficient. In a sense, financial delegation, the per-capita funding formula, self-governing schools, and open enrollment are merely the horses pulling on the choice cart.

Why did the Conservative government embrace choice? In part to empower parents. "Extending parents' rights and responsibilities, including their right of choice, will help raise standards by giving them greater influence over education," declared the Conservatives' manifesto in 1979. Later, a 1987 circular stated: "The opportunity for parents and the local community to run their own schools with funding direct from the central government will increase choice within the state sector."[1]

But other factors—factors particular to England's social history and its economy—led the government to extol the benefits of a more competitive school model. One was the rising cost of public services, which forced Prime Minister Margaret Thatcher to review state education in the early 1980s. The Conservatives wanted to curb spending and make schooling, like welfare services, more efficient. "Value for money" became their rallying cry. Subjecting schools to the forces of the market, they believed, would force educators to pay more attention to costs.

At the same time, demography was having a strong impact on government policy. The post-war expansion of state schooling had ended by the 1980s. Falling birthrates led to a sharp decline of the school-age population, from more than 6 million in 1973 to 4.5 million in 1987. Local authorities were forced to eliminate surplus spaces and close schools—a politically volatile issue.

But it wasn't feasible or practical to close *all* underused schools; the needs of the future remained uncertain. It fell to the localities, therefore, to regulate a system in which there were more spaces than pupils. While parents had the nominal right to choose any school within their district, the local authorities continued to exercise considerable discretionary power when assigning students. They tried to prevent popular schools from becoming overcrowded and unpopular schools from becoming inefficiently small.[2] They also engaged in a bit of social engineering, by balancing students' abilities within each school.

The Conservative government objected to this regulatory hand. It wanted to ensure that parents' demands were met and that the market, not the school managers, dictated the rolls. As one government document put it: "No child should be refused admission to a school unless it is genuinely full. . . . But in too many cases, parents are disappointed because artificial ceilings are set on the number of places available at popular schools. This barrier needs to be removed."[3]

Open enrollment offered a political solution that favored the parents over the local authorities. The provision, which establishes a "standard number" of pupils for each school, severely restricts the districts' ability to regulate intakes. Schools must now admit as many students as they can physically accommodate.

Finally, a bit of history helps to put parental choice in perspective. It was not until the mid-twentieth century that England began to unify a diverse and fragmented system of denominational and state schools. The 1944 Butler Act, which established free compulsory schooling for children five to fifteen, was really a religious settlement permitting denominational schools to receive public funds. In declaring that children should be educated "in accordance with the wishes of their parents," the wartime government recognized the historic role of church schools in British education.

In other ways, however, the post-war education system restricted parental choice by institutionalizing a "tripartite" system that included academically selective grammar schools, "secondary modern" schools, and a smattering of vocational, or technical, schools. Localities sorted and assigned students of differing abilities to the three categories. Inevitably, this academic segregation perpetuated a social segregation as well. Children of unskilled workers had a slim chance of securing a space in the more rigorous grammar schools, while children of professional workers had a better-than-even chance.[4]

In 1966, the government, well aware that selection at age eleven was unpopular with parents, began to dismantle the tripartite system. Most districts converted their schools into comprehensives. The conversion was steady and swift: in 1971, 35 percent of children in state schools attended comprehensive schools; by 1981, the figure was more than 90 percent.[5] The comprehensive movement significantly changed the culture of schooling and, according to compelling evidence, led to rising achievement among the working class.[6]

But comprehensive schools came in for criticism—and still do. Conservative policymakers were blunt in their attacks, suggesting that comprehensives had tipped the balance between excellence and equity too far in equity's favor. Comprehensives, in their view, represented a leveling down, rather than a leveling up, of state education. As Kenneth Baker and others saw it, a measure of choice and diversity had disappeared with the grammar schools and the demise of the tripartite system.

Grant-maintained schools and city technology colleges were devised in part to remedy the perceived inadequacies of the comprehensives. By distributing funds directly to schools threatened with closure or reorganization, the government hoped to circumvent local control and save the few grammar schools that remained—and any other schools that sought autonomy from their districts. Opting out would give parents an "escape route," advocates argued.[7]

This, then, is the historical backdrop for school choice in England. How is the scene playing today? Are parents satisfied with their choices? What do they look for in a school? What hinders choice? What effect has the more competitive market had on schools? Has it raised academic standards?

We begin at the Burntwood School for girls in south London.

Prospective parents and their daughters stream into the halls for the first of the fall season's "open evenings." Burntwood students, sporting red carnations and matching sweaters, are on hand to escort families to their seats. In the auditorium, brochures are stacked on tables, a video of a recent student production runs continuously in the corner, and teachers stand at attention next to large bulletin boards displaying information on the curricular programs. The atmosphere is that of a corporate convention. Eventually about five hundred people assemble to hear the principal, Brigid Beattie, talk about the school, explain its admissions procedures, and answer questions. A science teacher standing on the sidelines is blunt about the purpose of such an evening: "Students go to schools that put on shows like this," she says.

Open evenings are a pretty good setting to "see" choice in action. This is the time for parents and their children to gather information about the schools they're interested in, tour the classrooms, and talk to teachers. "It's important to look at lots of schools," one woman, poring over leaflets, told us. "I wouldn't want to have no choice." As families mill around the room, it's hard not to think of the market stalls on the village high streets. These people have come to shop and compare.

Many were looking at Burntwood two full years before the application deadline—"So that next year, we're not under pressure," as one parent put it. "Pressure," in fact, was a word on the lips of lots of parents. "It's awful going 'round them all," one mother says of the many school visits, both in and out of the borough, she and her husband have made over the years. "There are added pressures on parents right now."

"It's like roulette," one father told us. "It puts a lot of pressure on parents."

Nevertheless, few would return to the days when children were assigned to secondary schools.

Burntwood lies in the London borough of Wandsworth, a middle-class, multicultural neighborhood that has come to exemplify the new scholastic marketplace in England. Of eleven secondary schools, just three are maintained by the local authority; one is administered in partnership with the Church of England; six, including Burntwood, opted out of local control; finally, there is a city technology college. In such a setting, it's the authority's job to disseminate information about all the schools. The brochure "Choose a Wandsworth School" describes the options, outlines admissions criteria, and helps families navigate through the open evenings, interviews, aptitude tests, and application deadlines. It's up to parents and students to do the rest.

Donald Naismith, who recently stepped down as director of education in the borough, is a champion of choice. He told us that the "romantic notion" of the neighborhood school never really existed in Wandsworth. As elsewhere in England, the church schools exerted a powerful influence, and it was difficult for the authority to plan an equitable allocation of places, especially as the school-age population began to fall. Councillor Elizabeth Howlett described the standard of local schools as "pretty poor" before the borough embraced choice and scholastic diversity.

Today, Wandsworth parents can select from single-sex schools and co-ed schools; from among church schools, grant-maintained schools, and comprehensive schools; from schools that specialize in technology, in art and design, and in modern languages. Almost every secondary in the district has some form of selection, even if "selection" means admitting students of average aptitude and ability. "We see selection not as an issue of success or failure but as a means of matching child to school," Naismith explained.

Back at Burntwood, there's confusion and anxiety about the criteria for admission. "It's important parents understand the rules," says Howard Jackson, Burntwood's deputy principal. Every year, despite clear and categorical information in the school's prospectus, there are some parents who fail to fill out the requisite forms, believing spaces are guaranteed.

Burntwood chooses one-third of its incoming class on the basis of test scores. After that, preference will go to siblings and those living in the immediate neighborhood. The parents in the assembly hall are intent on the task ahead of them. Many questions concern the application procedure, the entrance examination, and the odds of gaining a space at this very popular secondary school.

"Everybody needs to make more than one application," warns Beattie, adding that it's "dangerously low" to have two choices. Parents get the message: there is no choice where there is no space. Preferred schools, such as Burntwood, fill up quickly.

What do parents think of choice in Wandsworth? By one measure, satisfaction with the borough's schools seems to be increasing. In 1990, 40 percent of local parents sought secondary education outside the district; in 1993, 25 percent did. Wandsworth parents have come to expect choice. At the same time, they've come to understand its limitations.

The Burntwood community's attitudes toward choice provide a pretty good barometer of attitudes nationwide, but data are scarce. Few organizations, whether governmental or private, have conducted surveys to determine just what parents and students actually think about the school marketplace. The evidence, therefore, remains largely anecdotal.

One of the most wide-ranging, ongoing investigations, the Parental and School Choice Interaction Study (PASCI) by researchers at the Open University, offers clues about parental reaction to the competitive schools market. Parents were polled in several representative districts—one urban, one suburban, and one rural. Majorities in each said they had a "real choice" among schools.[8] Not surprisingly, a greater proportion of parents from the urban district (72 percent) said they had a "real choice" than the proportion of parents from the rural district (56 percent). These figures contrast with significantly higher proportions of parents in both districts who say they obtained their "first choice," an issue we discuss in more detail later. What explains the discrepancy? Prof. Ron Glatter, who directs the Open University research study, points out that parents' "first choice" is often the easiest choice—the closest available school. Asking parents whether they have a range of "real choices" is different from asking them whether they secured their "first choice." Hence, the perception of choice varies depending on the precise question put to parents.

It's obvious that choice engages parents and their children. A typical family looking at secondary schools attends many open evenings, visits classrooms, reads numerous brochures, talks to friends and neighbors, reviews school data, and chooses from among three or even more institutions.[9] At Burntwood, we met scores of parents who were looking at six, seven, and even eight schools. "I want to get a feel for what's around, then narrow it down to four," one father explained.

The search for an appropriate school, whether elementary or secondary, culminates in the late fall, when most authorities require parents to list their preferences. Parents applying to grant-maintained schools must submit forms directly to the grant-maintained schools. Decisions are mailed in the spring. Families denied their first choice can then appeal.

Those who come through this lengthy admissions process successfully tend to feel good about the choices they make. As one parent told us: "Parents, having chosen a school, become even more supportive than otherwise. They're motivated to make it work." "The chosen schools get better," one Burntwood parent told us, "because the parents support them."

What are parents looking for in a school? In the 1992 Carnegie report on school choice, we observed that nonacademic criteria are as important—often more important—than strictly academic ones. The same is true in England. Parents tend to look first at a school's character—whether it is a denominational school or single-sex, for instance.[10] Beyond these attributes, families care about a school's location and convenience, its facilities, disciplinary policies, extracurricular programs *and* its academic reputation, according to studies of choice in London and elsewhere. Parents attending the Burntwood open evening wanted to know about the disciplinary procedures, about the extracurricular activities, and whether girls perform better at single-sex schools.

Philip Woods, one of the principal researchers for the Parental and School Choice Interaction Study, observes: "Nonacademic criteria are of great importance to parents. These include the child's perception of how secure he or she will feel in the school, the significance of friendship networks and the range of nonacademic curricular opportunities."[11]

It's worth noting that the British government has put a premium on the publication of school-by-school examination results, touting the data as crucial to parents' decision making. But according to parent surveys and interviews with headteachers, raw test scores mean less to parents than a multitude of other factors. Just 11 percent cited test scores as one of the three most important factors in choosing a school, according to one survey.[12]

In traveling the country, we found that the impact of choice on parents and their children varies tremendously. Much depends on the complex interplay of such factors as geography, the availability of school places in the most competitive arenas, and social class.

There's a saying that all politics is local; the same might be said of school choice. In metropolitan areas, such as greater London, parents have become accustomed to having choices. Indeed, the high concentration of schools made the metropolis a "choice district" long before the passage of the Education Reform Act. "I've always been conscious of parental choice," one headteacher told us. "We've always been in competition across the city." A headteacher in the outer London borough of Greenwich said: "There have always been popular and unpopular schools. There's always been cross-border activity." In the London metropolis, then, open enrollment and per-capita funding have merely accentuated the competition and raised parental expectations.

On the other hand, in the rural stretches of such counties as Northumberland, open enrollment is of little consequence. As in any choice scheme, long distances present a formidable barrier. We heard the story of a group of children living on the Scottish border. For them, a trip to school entails traveling by tractor, car, taxi, minivan, and finally double-decker bus. There are no other options.

Even in more densely populated counties, we learned that parents often select what are, in effect, their neighborhood schools, particularly when their children are young. County schools continue to serve students within defined boundaries. "Our schools serve catchment areas; movement is limited," explained Keith Anderson, Gloucestershire's chief education officer. The situation is the same in other shires, or English counties, according to administrators and teachers. This pattern parallels that of statewide choice programs in the United States. Clearly, there are limitations on the distances parents are willing to send their children, as well as limitations on the distances children themselves are willing to travel. Transportation often proves the obstacle; most authorities offer bus service only to schools in the family's catchment area. Open enrollment hasn't erased all boundary lines.

Geography is but one constraint; another is availability. School choice and the competitive model rest on the assumption that the most sought-after schools will expand. But where demand exceeds supply, the school market is unlike commercial markets. Once classrooms fill up, the coveted spaces must be rationed. Schools then choose students. The result is often disappointment for parents and students alike. It's no surprise that those who complain of having the fewest choices are often the very same parents and students who were denied spaces at their preferred schools.

Burntwood's deputy principal, Howard Jackson, is frank about parents' chances in Wandsworth: "If you like your local school, you're fine. If not, you've got a problem." Burntwood, because it is so popular, has few spaces for those living beyond a two-mile radius of the grounds. "Overall," concludes Mr. Jackson, "there's not a lot of satisfaction. . . . There's the expectation that they've got a choice and then there isn't a choice."

Competition among parents for the most coveted spaces can be fierce. The Hinchingbrooke School, the alma mater of Oliver Cromwell and Samuel Pepys among others, offers a case in point. It is the popular choice among the predominately middle-class residents of the town of Huntingdon, in Cambridgeshire. Each year sixty to one hundred students are turned away from the three-hundred-plus entry class. The local authority, which administers admissions, gives preference to siblings and to those who live closest to the school. Peter Downes, the headteacher, said some parents resort to ruses to get their children in, including claiming fake addresses. He's even been offered bribes, he says.

While nine out of ten students overall end up where they and their parents want them to go, according to one survey, the figures can vary wildly from locality to locality. In one London borough, for instance, just 60 percent were granted their first choice.[13] Further, the *London Times* found that "significantly fewer parents found places for their children in their first choice of secondary school" in 1993 than in 1992.[14] According to the Association of Metropolitan Authorities, *fewer* parents secure places at the schools of their choice now than before the passage of the Education Reform Act.[15] The data suggest the government's attempt to expand choice has been problematic in some areas.

Indeed, we met many for whom "school choice" was a false promise. Government rhetoric has led parents to "*think* they have more choices," according to Burntwood's principal, Brigid Beattie. In the words of another headteacher, "parental choice has caused a lot of aggravation, chaos and confusion." That confusion is reflected in the statistics on parental appeals—the administrative procedure used to address the grievances of parents. Appeals have increased steadily in many jurisdictions since 1988. One London borough, population 170,000, reported an explosion of appeals between 1989 and 1992, from 81 to 270.[16] Clearly, parental expectations are rising, and many confuse the right to state a preference with the right to attend the school of one's choice.

Finally, within the varied "landscapes of choice," we learned that different groups of parents exercise quite different options. Those who express preferences for schools outside their immediate neighborhood tend to be more highly educated and have more prestigious occupations than those who express a preference for their neighborhood school. In part, this phenomenon may be explained by the resources (money, transportation, information) available to more advantaged families, but we also found that the choices families make have much to do with cultural and ethnic values.

In Wandsworth and adjacent districts, for example, researchers from the University of London observe distinct "circuits of schooling," with different socioeconomic groups plugging into the various circuits. The "local community comprehensive" schools that recruit the majority of their students from the immediate neighborhood define one circuit. The "cosmopolitan, high-profile elite" schools that recruit from outside the area constitute another circuit. The Catholic schools are a third circuit. And the independent (that is, private) schools are yet another.[17]

In this setting, different social classes use the market differently. Middleclass parents are the more active strategists, while working class parents tend to identify strongly with the schools in their own immediate neighborhoods. "What we find is that a subsection of middle-class parents is very keen on choice," sociologist Stephen Ball told us. By contrast, working class parents aren't so keen. "They want a school as part of the local community. They put a value on that. Often the local school is the one that friends and relatives go to."

Similarly, the Parental and School Choice Interaction Study (PASCI) looked at a town of one hundred thousand with six publicly funded secondary schools. Questionnaires and interviews point to the vastly different priorities of parents. Most working class families express a preference for a nearby school. Middle-class and professional parents tend to seek more aggressively a school with a good academic reputation, though proximity is also high on their list.[18] And another investigation of a typical English county found that the more educated the mother and/or father and the higher-status jobs they had, the less likely they were to express a preference for their local school. Parents at the low end of the "social status index" preferred their local school 67 percent of the time, in comparison with 23 percent at the top end.[19]

Does this mean that professional and middle-class families have more choices than other families? Probably not. In the PASCI study, for instance, three-quarters of working class parents in one district considered they had a choice, compared with just over half of professional and middle-class parents.[20] But there is increasing evidence to suggest that the strategy *appeals* more to middle-class parents, that they "play the market" more avidly than participants from other socio-economic groups, and that their expectations are higher. They assume their preferences will be honored.

Policymakers in the United States would do well to take note of this evidence. It challenges the long-held supposition that the poor and disadvantaged will benefit most by choice. In 1992, when we looked at school choice in American communities, we found that choice works best for the more affluent, better educated parents. The same appears to be true in England.[21]

So FAR, WE'VE LOOKED at how parents use choice and the competitive market. It's also essential to look at the strategy from the schools' perspective. Just as there is competition among parents for the preferred spaces, there is also competition—ruthless, in some cases—among schools for students. The reason is that the delegation of budgets and the per-capita funding formula force schools to go after students in order to go after money. "Every child is worth a sum of money," points out the chief education officer of Birmingham, Tim Brighouse. "It used not to matter if there were a few more or a few less. Now kids are a kind of bounty."

The challenge to schools is amply illustrated by the case of Wright Robinson High School in Manchester, where the loss of just ten pupils can mean a cut of $37,500 from the school budget, a figure that represents the cost of employing more than one teacher.

Writing in the *Times Educational Supplement*, headteacher Neville Beischer explains: "We are on the eastern side of Manchester and have some fifteen secondary schools within a two-and-a-half mile radius, many of which are competing for a share of the pupils who live locally. Our neighbors include two of the top independent schools in the country, two single-sex ex-grammars (both grant-maintained), three Catholic comprehensives and eight other comprehensives, including my own. It would be nice to believe that Wright Robinson's good reputation would be enough to ensure a full intake each September. However, I realize that the drive by many of the schools around us to recruit pupils is gathering pace all the time. My school, the largest eleven-to-sixteen in the city, has to fill more than three hundred places each September—this cannot be left to chance."[22]

Wright Robinson has developed its own strategy for attracting prospective eleven-year-olds and their parents. The school begins each academic year by building a register of all potential candidates from the local primary schools; opening the school's swimming pool to these children; offering special sports courses; inviting the youngsters into the school; distributing brochures and school newspapers to the feeder primaries; writing welcome letters to prospective parents; offering tours and interviews; and so forth. Recruitment, in other words, amounts to utilizing an array of sophisticated marketing techniques.

This is by no means unusual. Choice cannot succeed without adequate information. Most governing bodies now have marketing committees, and schools are spending considerable sums and much administrative capital on producing brochures, distributing glossy prospectuses, and garnering public relations advice. The reforms have led to a veritable information explosion. The government requires each school to publish its "vital statistics" in a yearly prospectus, and governors must issue an annual report to parents. A prospectus describes something about the school's ethos, admissions procedures, how many parents applied for places in the previous year, and how many pupils were admitted. It includes examinations results, rates of unauthorized absence, and so on. Headteachers and their staffs understand the importance of communicating their missions to prospective parents. "When schools market themselves, they look for their sense of identity," Burntwood's headteacher, Brigid Beattie, said.

K. H. Brooke, headteacher of The Garth Hill School in suburban Berkshire, says information is vital in her school market, where there are four other secondaries, including two single-sex schools that in "some parents' minds are better" and a "school down the road that's got a name—Ascot." Garth Hill puts out a glossy prospectus and conducts an information evening, an open house, and a "principal's question time" every term. "It's helpful to walk parents around. We've hyped it up, gotten quite professional, adopted a house style. . . . When parents choose, we have to have an eye to what the opposition is doing."

Schools are also responding to market pressures by altering their curricular programs, teaching methods, admissions policies, management styles, and so forth.[23] Most of the decisions appear to be financially driven. The schools, to use the jargon, are trying to increase their "market share," to draw in more pupils. Many are attempting to appeal to parents by reintroducing uniforms, for instance, or by offering new courses. Grant-maintained schools, as we noted in the previous chapter, are becoming selective. It's unclear whether schools are responding directly to what parents want or to what they think parents want. Either way, the competitive forces are compelling many schools to examine their programs and policies more carefully. "Schools are having to pick themselves up by the bootstraps. They have to think about discipline, ethos—that's a positive thing," one parent commented.

But many complain that the marketing of education has gone too far.

Some schools advertise on billboards and on radio. A few have even resorted to "attack ads," in which they put down their chief rivals. Others have lured prospective students by promising gifts once they enroll. One school, for instance, struck a $30,000 deal with a local savings and loan to provide free notebooks. Another offered cases containing pens, pencils, erasers, rulers, and other paraphernalia. In Warwickshire, a school governor offered 10 percent off on bathroom fittings from his local store to all parents who enrolled their children.[24]

Still others question the resources spent on annual reports and slick brochures, which tend to paint a partial—and sometimes distorted—picture of a school. In the end, parents rely more on their own observations during school visits and on what they've heard from friends and neighbors. In one survey, just half the respondents said they used the brochures at all.[25] "Parents choose a school on the basis of what other parents say predominately," Peter Downes, of Hinchingbrooke School, told us. "I put the parental relationship right at the top of my priorities—that's my main marketing tool."

Finally, while choice may force some schools to "pick themselves up by their bootstraps" and to pay closer attention to the essential service they are providing, there is no evidence that competition among schools leads to higher educational standards overall. In fact, the strategy, backed by the cudgel of per-capita funding, tends to widen the gap between good and bad, between rich and poor. Since per-pupil expenditures are higher in small schools than in large ones, England's choice scheme punishes schools with falling rolls. A Burntwood parent stated the dilemma succinctly: "Choice has ranked schools. Some are very good, others aren't."

We visited undersubscribed schools where the loss of pupils and the concomitant loss of funds had put an end to remedial programs and extracurricular activities. In such circumstances, schools not only lose their ability to help their own students; they also lose the ability to compete.[26]

In England survival of the fittest means survival of the fullest; those schools that enroll the most students are the schools most likely to thrive. But schools don't necessarily lose students because parental opinion has turned against them. The local school-age population may drop, or a factory may close, forcing families to move elsewhere. Schools in small rural communities or near public housing sites in troubled inner cities are particularly vulnerable to the migration of a small number of pupils.[27]

Schools with diminishing rolls not only lose resources; they lose pride, too. As the headteacher of the Geoffrey Chaucer School in London's tough Southwark neighborhood explained, the government's choice program has caused "more pressure on already pressurized schools." Chaucer has a transient student population, and therefore an unstable budget. In the past years it has lost funds for special needs classes, teachers of English as a second language, and the on-site unit for students with behavioral problems, all because it's been losing the numbers game.

The Peers School, in the outskirts of Oxford, is trying to reverse years of declining enrollment caused primarily by migration out of the neighboring public housing site. In January 1988, the school enrolled 850 students and employed a staff of 65; by 1994–95, the rolls had fallen to 547 students and 33 staff members. "You can see how a school in this location, surrounded by other schools in more favored locations, could go to the wall," said headteacher Bernard Clarke.

But Peers is "bucking the counterforces," as Clarke put it. In recent years, despite falling enrollments, low test scores, and a decimated staff, the school has managed to attract students from outside the immediate neighborhood. "Parents had looked around," said Clarke. What they find is a disciplined yet spirited school that provides plenty of enrichment activities—financed in part by local industry, private benefactors, and fund-raising. The Education Plus program, for instance, offers tutoring to kids after school hours. A public library and a further education center, both on campus, lure others from the community into the school.

Clarke says his mission is to persuade the middle classes that, if they take the risk, they will receive as good an education at Peers as at the better endowed, more popular school a few miles away, Cherwell. ("In Oxford city," Clarke explains, "choice means whether or not you can get into Cherwell.") He works closely with the junior high schools to recruit students. "We know our budget is based on however many we get. To be an underfunded downmarket school doesn't do us any good," he says.

A few miles away, off the leafy avenues that radiate from Oxford University's college campuses, the Cherwell school commands a prime location. But it too has problems. Cherwell's enrollment rose from 639 in 1981 to 965 in 1994–95. The school has become a victim of its own success. Eighteen temporary classrooms are crowded around the original school building. As headmaster Martin Roberts awaits construction of permanent buildings, he doubts whether bigger is necessarily better. "If we take another ninety pupils a year that would mean ninety fewer going to other schools, to which they are probably living closer. If we did that I think one of the six other secondaries in Oxford would have to close," he said.[28]

Advocates of the competitive choice model might cheer such an outcome. But so far, market forces have dictated neither a rash of closures nor a building boom at the most sought-after schools. In fact, head-teachers at oversubscribed schools resist expansion. "I try to get this school running at its most cost-effective size," Peter Downes, at Hinchingbrooke, told us. "When it's too big, you lose quality. There comes a point beyond which schools should not go."

Before we leave school choice in England, it's worthwhile to take a detour to Scotland, where parental choice was expanded in 1982. The evidence from more than a decade of open enrollment suggests that the strategy has led to marked differences between schools. Schools that lost pupils lost staff and resources and could no longer offer comparable educational opportunities. In Scotland's big cities, choice has led to the emergence of a two-tiered system and the existence of "rump schools" in the most deprived inner-city areas, according to well-documented research.

Sociologist Michael Adler at the University of Edinburgh sums it up this way: "Although there have clearly been gainers as well as losers from the Scottish legislation, the balance sheet suggests that the gains have been relatively small compared with the losses. Those who have gained have done so at the expense of others and, by and large, those who have lost have been those who could least afford to do so. Thus, parental choice in Scotland appears to have been a 'negative sum' game in which the gains achieved by some pupils have been more than offset by the losses incurred by others and by the community as a whole."[29]

Will the long-term impact of parental choice in England parallel the impact in Scotland? Many fear so. If the children of more educated and economically advantaged families are seeking the more popular schools with the better reputations, then these schools are likely to succeed. They will receive the financial support of the state and the social support of the parents and children. Sir John Cassells, who directed a national education commission that looked at the effects of choice, is pessimistic: "From the point of view of society, choice stratifies," he said.

The Organization for Economic Cooperation and Development also emphasizes the propensity of choice to rank schools. Its 1994 worldwide survey of choice programs concludes: "Perhaps the biggest problem with school choice in England is the national habit of ranking educational alternatives rather than seeing them as being of possibly equal value. This potential makes school choice an exercise in which for every winner there is a loser. The pluralistic attitude to education evident in the Netherlands and Denmark, and in some contexts in the United States, seems unlikely to take root easily in England."[30]

National habits are hard to break. In England, the competitive choice model seems to perpetuate the stratifications evident throughout the society—stratifications that the post-war welfare state did not dismantle. The benefits of choice seem to appear on the margins. Open enrollment forces parents to think about what schools are best for their children, and it compels schools to think hard about their clients and their programs. But the strategy also raises expectations, creates confusion, and leads to disappointment. It is not spurring the creation of academically superior schools overall. Rather, it is recreating a pecking order, in which the least popular are the least able to improve and compete.

CHAPTER IV

The Picture of Reform

INDIVIDUAL SNAPSHOTS don't necessarily reveal the big picture. It's important to remember that the national curriculum, local management, self-governing schools, open enrollment, and per-capita funding fit together in a reform puzzle along with other pieces—teacher training and school inspection, for instance—that are missing from this study. Assemble them all and what you see is a very different system of elementary and secondary education from the one that existed in England a decade ago. The post-war institutional framework for state schooling was knocked down. The new framework has a different architecture. The old social democratic approach, with its emphasis on collaboration, has been replaced by a market-oriented model, with an emphasis on competition and parent power.

The effect is paradoxical. The central government exerts more control than it once did, but so do the hundreds of thousands of laymen who serve as school governors. The local education authorities, while forced to relax their hold over budgets, personnel, planning, and student admissions, nevertheless play a vital mediating and strategic planning role. The system that emerges is more diverse; but expectations for achievement are more uniform.

The reforms raise more questions than they answer. How is power to be shared among the central government, the local authorities, and the schools? Can schools—both locally maintained and grant-maintained—manage without strong regional coordination? Will political appointees continue to steer the national curriculum with the consent of the teachers? Can the government conscript commitment from parents and other lay representatives?

As the government and schools continue to assemble this reform puzzle, the picture remains unclear. There is little evidence that the national curriculum, local management, grant-maintained schools, and school choice have significantly raised standards. Yet many of the changes—notably the need to create a national framework for the curriculum and the delegation of decision making—have received the support of the profession and parents alike. Even the two major political parties are narrowing their differences, with Labor conceding the advantages of local management and delegated funding. A recent poll found that 83 percent of parents were satisfied with state secondary education, up from 73 percent in 1987. At the same time, however, just one in four parents thought the changes had helped to raise standards.[1]

What do we see from England? We conclude our study with these thoughts:

Statehouses and school boards seeking to raise curriculum standards must seek the advice and willing participation of teachers and parents.

In England, the national curriculum became primarily an instrument of politics, rather than of education. Government ministers formulated standards without sufficient consideration of the people most affected by the mandates. The voices of classroom teachers, as well as those of students and parents, were ignored. The mistake cost the central government time, trust, and considerable sums of money. Had the School Curriculum and Assessment Authority conducted as thorough a consultation in 1988 as it did in 1993–94, the first curriculum would have been written differently and its chances of success might have been better.

The United States will not adopt a national curriculum, nor will the Department of Education exert power over the local schools as many European central ministries do. Still, statehouses would do well to heed the lesson from London. Education policies cannot—and should not—be made without regard to the key constituencies in the schools. In too many communities, and in too many capital committee rooms, a blame-the-teacher attitude hampers reform. The curriculum is too important to become caught in the politics of division. When it comes to establishing standards in the core subjects, teachers must play a leading role. Their advice must be heard, and their experience must be respected.

A carefully crafted curriculum framework can help, rather than hinder, teachers.

Teachers want and need considerable freedom and flexibility in the classroom, but they and their students can also benefit from a set of clearly articulated expectations for both teaching and learning—expectations shared inside the school and outside it, throughout the greater community. The best curriculum standards represent a kind of contract between teacher and student, between school and society. They help define the goals of education.

While teachers in England don't always agree with the School Curriculum and Assessment Authority, or with particular aspects of the various curricula, there is little doubt that the curriculum documents themselves have introduced an unprecedented interest in a wide variety of subject matter and in the key stages of learning. Teachers have used the curriculum as a national discussion document; it has led them to examine more closely their own approach to teaching and to think more carefully about textbooks, resources, and what students ought to know. This impromptu exercise has proved invaluable.

We believe the emerging curriculum standards and curriculum frameworks in the United States have the potential to perform a similar function. The mathematics standards formulated by the National Council of Teachers of Mathematics already have spurred math teachers across the country to revise their lesson plans and to think more carefully about what arithmetical skills and mathematical principles students should know. Standards in other subjects, though more difficult to agree on, could have a similar effect. The evidence suggests that curriculum standards can liberate, rather than bind, teachers and students alike.

New assessment techniques must be piloted, well funded, and supported by education's various constituents. Their purpose must be stated with precision.

Measuring and comparing achievement means assessment. Increasing pressure for higher achievement will mean increasing pressure for better assessment. The challenges are immense in a highly technical field not well understood by the public.

England embarked on a bold experiment for which its students, teachers, parents, and politicians were unprepared. The experts' vision of an integrated system of continuous teacher assessment coupled with standardized national tests using performance tasks has so far failed to become a reality. Teachers resented the administrative burden, as well as the government's intention to use the results to compare individual schools. Parents were confused about the standardized tests and worried about the effects of assessing children as young as seven. The government failed to anticipate the objections. A simpler scheme has now been advanced.

In this country, districts and states are beginning to take a broader view of assessment; many are moving away from multiple-choice tests whose primary purpose is to rank and sort students. They are measuring achievement by assembling portfolios of student work and by giving written and oral examinations. In some states, the scores are now based on performance criteria rather than on student averages.

Whatever the particular testing program, it is important to know precisely what its purpose is. Are the results meant to help teachers and parents diagnose students' capabilities or to make comparative judgments about schools and their districts? In England, the conflation of purposes led to both technical and political obstacles. So far, national testing has tended to foster a consumerist, rather than educational, interest in student achievement.[2]

Assessment must enhance learning. It should aid both the teachers and their students. Hastily designed testing programs that attempt solely to satisfy political demands for public accountability aren't likely to succeed.

Local management and financial delegation offer schools the flexibility to tailor resources to particular needs.

Decisions that most affect a school are best made within that school. In England, decisions about spending, staffing, and planning are made by the headteacher and a team of teacher-managers. The result has been that more resources flow to the classroom. Schools are spending more, as a percentage of their total budget, on teachers' aides, books, materials, and technological improvements. Schools generally appear cleaner and brighter than before the introduction of local management, because refurbishments aren't delayed. Perhaps most important, schools that manage themselves tend to take more pride in themselves.

The record of local management in England offers compelling evidence that devolution can spur substantial improvements. We'd like to see more school districts within the United States assign greater budgetary and planning authority to principals and teachers. While local management is not a funding strategy that ensures equitability, it is an administrative strategy with great potential.

Self-governing schools run the risk of threatening a planned and integrated system of education dedicated to equal access.

Autonomy has its merits, but schools serve the public best when they collaborate within a regional system dedicated to a common purpose. In England, there is growing concern that the grant-maintained sector, though still relatively small, encourages selection and elitism. If GM schools adopt enrollment policies that are more restrictive than those of other local schools, then primary and secondary education is likely to become more fragmented, leading to a two-tier system of best and second-best.

In the United States, there is a growing interest in new organizational models. Will the growing number of charter schools lead to a similar fragmentation within and among American school districts? What does it portend when private management consultants take over ailing public schools? Whatever the answers, the strategies for better school administration and responsive governance must not eclipse the commitment to equal access for all, one of the hallmarks of American public education.

The quest for greater autonomy within schools must not jeopardize accountability to democratically elected institutions.

Many reformers, notably John E. Chubb and Terry M. Moe, have advanced the proposition that the schools' most fundamental problems are rooted in the institutions of democratic control. Bureaucratization and centralization, they contend, impede effectiveness and innovation.

Perhaps. But America's schools, if they are to serve the public well, must remain accountable to institutions of government.

That message rings out clearly from England, where reforms have led to an erosion of democratic accountability. Local education authorities, subsidiaries of local government, are no longer the major mediators of policy. Today, school governors—some of them appointed rather than elected—are on the front lines. Can these volunteers fairly resolve all conflicts within schools and among schools? Who will address disputes between parents and governing bodies? Between governing bodies and the central government? In a few cases, LEAs have been forced to intervene where there is evidence of managerial incompetence or misconduct. These isolated incidents suggest the continued need for government oversight.

There are limits to parental choice.

England's Conservative Party extols the power of parents to choose their children's schools. But the reality is somewhat different from the rhetoric. Most students continue to attend their local neighborhood schools. Those who do exercise their right to state a preference for a school outside their neighborhood soon discover the constraints. As we've noted in this report, availability of school places, selective admissions policies, locale, and social class all have a bearing on the outcome. In the most competitive arenas, such as greater London, schools are more likely to choose students than students are to choose schools. This is the case wherever space is rationed. The schools market, therefore, is not like other markets. Demand rarely matches supply. The result often leads to confusion, frustration, and disappointment.

Per-capita funding and a competitive market force schools to become rivals striving to gain advantage.

We are reminded of Birmingham's chief education officer, Tim Brighouse, who offered this trenchant comment: "Every child is worth a sum of money. It used not to matter if there were a few more or a few less. Now kids are a kind of bounty."

In many areas of the country, the per-capita budget formula instituted to promote school choice in fact promotes competition for students and the money each brings. To be sure, competition can have beneficial effects on some schools and their administration. Too often, though, the race for students boosts some schools at the expense—quite literally—of others. Oversubscribed schools in England are, for the most part, financially stable and educationally sound. Undersubscribed schools, on the other hand, are not. With the fall in students comes a dramatic and deleterious decline in funding and resources. The consequence is not to expand the range of acceptable choices but to restrict it.

Change should be implemented for educational advantage, not political expediency.

By the 1980s, pressure to reform British schooling was intense. An unprecedented expansion of primary and secondary education had been followed by doubts about teaching methods, the curriculum, and discipline, as well as concern over the steep rise in cost. The government, as well as the public, demanded accountability for a system that seemed at times to satisfy itself rather than parents, students, and employers.

The Conservative Party, perhaps unsurprisingly, adopted an interventionist approach. The 1988 Education Reform Act mandated far-reaching changes at the school, district, and national levels. Reformers were as keen to act in the name of efficiency as in the name of effectiveness.

Today, many bemoan the consequences of such rapid-fire reform. The national curriculum, the assessment program, and many of the regulations pertaining to self-governing schools were instituted without sufficient consultation or field research. A member of the University of Oxford Department of Educational Studies writes: "Government strategies have been predicated to a substantial degree on assumptions that its policies for parental choice and local management of schools were attractive to parents and, consequently, that it would gain widespread support for the entire package of its mandated reforms. Characteristically, the government failed to test these assumptions in the early years of reform and, as change has proceeded in hyper-drive during the past five years, clear signs of innovation-fatigue and resistance to unbridled political change are now emerging."[3]

England serves as a warning bell for school boards, state legislators, and other policymakers eager to improve the schools quickly. They must listen, consult, and act without haste. Schools can't be reformed according to political timetables.

We hope these thoughts will guide educators in the United States as they seek—to come back to the words of Horace Mann—to avoid the "calamities" and imitate the "blessings" evident in other countries.

APPENDIX

APPENDIX

Site Visits

Primary Schools

Eric Spear, *Headteacher*
Staplehurst School
Staplehurst, Tonbridge

Michael Russell, *Headteacher*
Malmesbury Junior School
Bow, London

John Kenward, *Headteacher*
Bourne County Primary School
Eastbourne, East Sussex

Secondary Schools

Brigid Beattie, *Headteacher*
Burntwood School (grant-maintained)
London

Mike Read, *Headteacher*
Geoffrey Chaucer School
London

Martin Roberts, *Headteacher*
The Cherwell School
Oxford

Peter Hore, *Headteacher*
Eltham Green School
Eltham, London

Stephen Szemerenyi, *Headteacher*
Finchley Catholic High School
(grant-maintained)
London

K. H. Brooke, *Headteacher*
The Garth Hill School
Bracknell, Berkshire

Andrea Berkeley, *Deputy Head*
Hampstead High School
Hampstead, London

Peter Downes, *Headteacher*
Hinchingbrooke School
Huntingdon, Cambridgeshire

Michael Duffy, *Headteacher*
The King Edward VI School
Morpeth, Northumberland

Bernard Clarke, *Headteacher*
The Peers School
Littlemore, Oxfordshire

Local Education Authorities

Andrew Howell, *Chairman, Education Committee*
Birmingham City Council

Tim Brighouse, *Director of Education*
Birmingham

Peter Mitchell, *Director of Education*
Camden Council
London

Keith Anderson, *Chief Education Officer*
Gloucestershire County Council
Gloucestershire

Roy Pryke, *Chief Education Officer*
Kent County Council
Kent

Chris Tipple, *Director of Education*
Northumberland County Council

Donald Naismith, *Director of Education*
Wandsworth Council
London

Margaret Maden, *Chief Education Officer*
Warwickshire County Council

City Technology Colleges

Peter Jenkins, *Headteacher*
Bacon's College
Rotherhithe, London

Anne Rumney, *Headteacher*
Brit School
Croyden, Surrey

Clive Andrews, *Administrative Director*
City Technology Colleges Trust
London

Unions and Associations

John Sutton, *General Secretary*
Secondary Heads Association

Peter Smith, *General Secretary*
Association of Teachers and Lecturers
London

Arthur De Caux, *Senior Assistant Secretary*
National Association of Head Teachers

Other Organizations

Adrian Pritchard, *Director*
Grant-Maintained Schools Center
High Wycombe, Buckinghamshire

School Curriculum and Assessment Authority
London

Peter Newsam, *Director*
Institute of Education
University of London

J. R. G. Tomlinson, *Director*
Institute of Education
University of Warwick

Centre for Educational Studies
Kings College, London

Andrew McPherson, *Professor*
Centre for Educational Sociology
University of Edinburgh
Edinburgh, Scotland

Sir John Cassels, *Director*
National Commission on Education
London

NOTES

NOTES

CHAPTER 1   *Standards: Going for Control*

1. *Making Standards Matter: A 50-State Progress Report on Efforts to Raise Academic Standards* (Washington, D.C.: American Federation of Teachers, 1995).
2. Alex Medler, *Examples and Summaries of State Initiatives to Develop Goals, Standards and Outcomes* (Denver, CO: Education Commission of the States, May 1994).
3. Paul Black, "The Shifting Scenery of the National Curriculum," in *Assessing the National Curriculum*, Philip O'Hear and John White, eds. (London: Paul Chapman Publishing Ltd., 1993), 57.
4. John Tomlinson, *The Control of Education* (London: Cassell, 1993), 63.
5. *Ibid.*, 70–71.
6. *Ibid.*, 75.
7. Andy Green and Hilary Steedman, *Educational Provision, Educational Attainment and the Needs of Industry: A Review of Research from Germany, France, Japan, the USA and Britain*, Report Series No. 5 (London: National Institute of Economic and Social Research, 1993), 9.
8. Conversation with Prof. Michael Barber of Keele University, Staffordshire, England, January 1994.
9. These and subsequent citations from Education Reform Act 1988 (London: Her Majesty's Stationery Office, reprinted 1989).
10. Department for Education and the Office for Standards in Education, *The Government's Expenditure Plans, 1994–1995 to 1996–1997* (London: HMSO, 1994), 11.
11. See Institute for Public Policy Research, *Education: A Different Version* (London: Institute for Public Policy Research, 1993), 20; citing Julian Haviland's analysis of all 11,790 responses to the government's consultation paper on the 1988 bill and compiled in the book *Take Care, Mr. Baker!*
12. Stuart Maclure, *Education Re-Formed* (London: Hodder and Stoughton, 1992), vii.

13. Ron Dearing, *The National Curriculum and Its Assessment: Final Report* (London: School Curriculum and Assessment Authority, December 1993), 63.
14. Kenneth Baker, *The Turbulent Years: My Life in Politics* (London: Faber & Faber, 1993), 198.
15. Ron Dearing, *National Curriculum, Final Report.*
16. Ron Dearing, *The National Curriculum and Its Assessment, Interim Report* (London: School Curriculum and Assessment Authority, July 1993), 5.
17. *Ibid.*, 27.
18. Department of Education and Science, *In-Service Training for the Introduction of the National Curriculum: A Report by H M Inspectorate 1988–1990* (London: HMSO, 1991), 10.
19. Department for Education and the Office for Standards in Education, *The Government's Expenditure Plans, 1994–1995 to 1996–1997* (London: HMSO, 1994), 26–27.
20. Office for Standards in Education, *Geography: Key Stages 1, 2 and 3* (London: HMSO, 1993), 4.
21. National Union of Teachers, *The True Costs of the Curriculum,* London, April 1992, 6.
22. Office for Standards in Education, *Standards and Quality in Education, 1992–1993: The Annual Report of Her Majesty's Chief Inspector of Schools* (London: HMSO, 1993), 6.
23. *Ibid.*, 13.
24. Maureen O'Connor, "Teachers Forced to Bow to Tradition," *Times Educational Supplement*, 17 September 1993; and Fran Abrams, "Teachers 'Forced Back to Old Methods,'" *The Independent*, 12 September 1993.
25. Office for Standards in Education, *Standards and Quality*, 14.
26. Barbara MacGilchrist, "A Primary Perspective on the National Curriculum," in *Assessing the National Curriculum*, 120–21.
27. Office for Standards in Education, *Standards and Quality*, 19.
28. Michael Barber, "Teachers and the National Curriculum: Learning to Love It?" in *Sense, Nonsense and the National Curriculum*, Michael Barber and Duncan Graham, eds. (London: Falmer Press, 1993), 22–23.
29. *Ibid.*, 23–24.
30. Denis Lawton, "National Curriculum: Professional or Ideological?" in *Assessing the National Curriculum*, 41.

31. Alan Leech, "The National Curriculum in a Secondary School," in *Sense, Nonsense and the National Curriculum*, 57–58.
32. Paul Black, "Performance Assessment and Accountability: The Experience in England and Wales," *Educational Evaluation and Policy Analysis* 16, no. 2 (summer 1994).
33. Caroline Gipps, writing in *Curriculum Reform: Assessment in Question* (Paris: Organization for Economic Cooperation and Development, 1993), 109.
34. *Ibid.*, 109.
35. *Ibid.*, 118.
36. Dennie Palmer Wolf, Paul LeMahieu, and JoAnne Eresh, "Good Measure: Assessment as a Tool for Educational Reform," *Educational Leadership*, May 1992, 9.

CHAPTER II *Autonomy: Going It Alone*

1. Jane L. David, "School-Based Decision Making: Kentucky's Test of Decentralization," *Phi Delta Kappan*, May 1994, 706–12.
2. Elizabeth Monck and Alison Kelly, *Managing Effective Schools* (London: Institute for Public Policy Research, 1992), 2.
3. Peter Downes, ed., *Local Financial Management in Schools* (Oxford: Basil Blackwell, Ltd., 1988), 4.
4. Gwen Wallace, ed., *Local Management, Central Control* (Bournemouth: Hyde Publications, 1993), 13.
5. *Ibid.*, 94.
6. Cited in Stuart Maclure, *Education Re-Formed* (London: Hodder and Stoughton, 1992), 50.
7. Department for Education and Science, *Education Reform Act: Local Management of Schools* Circular 7/88 (London: Her Majesty's Stationery Office).
8. Department for Education, *The Implementation of Local Management of Schools: A Report by H M Inspectorate 1989-1992* (London: HMSO, 1993), 21.
9. Chris Emerson, *All About LMS* (London: Heinemann, 1991), 39–40.
10. Department for Education, *The Implementation of Local Management of Schools*.

11. Audit Commission, "Adding Up the Sums: Schools' Management of Their Finances," HMSO, London, 1993, 1.
12. Department for Education, *The Implementation of Local Management of Schools*, 19.
13. Gwen Wallace, 13, 93.
14. Stephen Ball, "Culture, Cost and Control: Self-Management and Entrepreneurial Schooling in England and Wales," report based on a symposium paper presented at the American Educational Research Association in San Francisco, 1992, 11.
15. *Ibid.*, 13.
16. Bob Doe, "Call for More Accountability," *Times Educational Supplement*, 11 November 1994.
17. Elizabeth Monck and Alison Kelly, *Managing Effective Schools*, iii.
18. Audit Commission, "Adding Up the Sums: Schools' Management of Their Finances," 25.
19. Michael Flude and Merrill Hammer, *The Education Reform Act, 1988: Its Origins and Implications* (London: Falmer Press, 1990), 164.
20. Stuart Maclure, 55.
21. According to the Audit Commission, it will be some years before enough pupils have spent sufficient time in schools that manage their own finances to judge LMS's contribution to improving education. Evaluation has been hindered by a lack of objective comparative information on financial management. See Audit Commission, "Adding Up the Sums: Schools' Management of Their Finances," HMSO, London, 1993.
22. Clare Dean, "GM Heads Fight for Moral High-Ground," *Times Educational Supplement*, 7 October 1994.
23. Clare Dean, "Opt-Out Heads Just Wanted to Be Free," *Times Educational Supplement*, 7 October 1994.
24. David Halpin, Sally Power, and John Fitz, "Opting Into State Control? Headteachers and the Paradoxes of Grant-Maintained Status," *International Studies in Sociology of Education* 3, no. 1, 1993, 15.
25. Cecil Knight, "A Case Study of Opting-Out: Small Heath School, Birmingham," in *Opting for Self-Management: The Early Experience of Grant-Maintained Schools*, Brent Davies and Lesley Anderson, eds. (London: Routledge, 1992), 27.
26. Local Schools Information, "Opting Out for What? A Choice for Parents," London, April 1994.

27. Office for Standards in Education, *Grant-Maintained Schools, 1989-1992* (London: HMSO, 1993), 12.
28. Some of Brigid Beattie's comments, gathered from drafts she submitted to us, were later published in *Towards Self-Managing Schools*, edited by Vivian Williams (London: Cassell, 1995), 111-23.
29. Tony Bush, Marianne Coleman, and Derek Glover, *Managing Autonomous Schools* (London: Paul Chapman Publishing, Ltd., 1993), 95.
30. Roy Pryke, "Opting Into Irrelevance," *Times Educational Supplement*, 1 October 1993.
31. David Halpin, John Fitz, and Sally Power, "Opting Into State Control? Headteachers and the Paradoxes of Grant-Maintained Status," *International Studies in Sociology of Education* 3, no. 1, 1993.
32. Clare Dean, "Forced to Follow in Enemy Footsteps," *Times Educational Supplement*, 19 June 1992.
33. Roy Pryke, "Opting Into Irrelevance."
34. From memo by Roy Pryke to the Kent County Education Committee, 4 October 1993, B3.3.
35. Roy Pryke, "Opting Into Irrelevance."
36. David Halpin, John Fitz, and Sally Power, *The Early Impact and Long-Term Implications of the Grant-Maintained Schools Policy* (Stoke-on-Trent: Trentham Books, 1993), 27.
37. Marianne Coleman, Tony Bush, and Derek Glover (1993) suggest in a survey of the first one hundred grant-maintained schools that only 4 percent of parents were advocates of GM status.
38. Local Schools Information, "Opting Out for What?"
39. John E. Chubb and Terry M. Moe, *A Lesson in School Reform from Great Britain* (Washington, D.C.: The Brookings Institution, 1992), 28.
40. Office for Standards in Education, *Standards and Quality in Education, 1992-1993: The Annual Report of Her Majesty's Chief Inspector of Schools* (London: HMSO, 1993), 24.
41. Geoff Turner, "More for Opt Outs Means Less for the Rest," Letters, *Times Educational Supplement*, 21 October 1994.
42. Kenneth Baker, *The Turbulent Years: My Life in Politics* (London: Faber & Faber, 1993), 177.
43. Julia Hagedorn, *The Longer School Day and Five-Term Year in CTCs* (London: CTC Trust, Ltd., 1992), 16.

44. Geoffrey Walford, *Choice and Equity in Education* (London: Cassell, 1994), 80.
45. Clare Dean, "High-cost CTCs Fall Short of Excellence," *Times Educational Supplement*, 25 November 1994.

CHAPTER III   *Choice: Going to Market*

1. Department for Education and Science, *Education Reform: The Government's Proposal for Schools* (London: HMSO, 1987), 15.
2. Stuart Maclure, *Education Re-Formed* (London: Hodder and Stoughton, 1992), 34–36.
3. Department for Education and Science, 8.
4. J. E. Floud, ed., A. H. Halsey, and F. M. Martin, *Social Class and Educational Opportunity* (London: Heinemann, 1956), 42.
5. Geoffrey Walford, "Selection for Secondary Schooling," National Commission on Education, Briefing No. 7 (London: National Commission on Education, October 1992).
6. *Ibid.*
7. Kenneth Baker, *The Turbulent Years: My Life in Politics* (London: Faber & Faber, 1993), 214–15.
8. Philip Woods, "Parents and Choice in Local Competitive Arenas: First Findings from the Main Phase of the PASCI Study," paper presented at the annual meeting of the American Educational Research Association, Atlanta, GA, April 1994, 4.
9. Anne West's research for the Centre for Educational Research at the London School of Economics was helpful in documenting how parents and their children choose schools. See *Choosing a Secondary School: The Parents' and Pupils' Stories* (London: London School of Economics, 1993).
10. Barry Bastow, "A Study of Factors Affecting Parental Choice of Secondary School," Ph.D. thesis for the Institute of Education, University of London, 1991.
11. Philip Woods, "Parental Perspectives on Choice in the United Kingdom," paper presented at the annual meeting of the American Educational Research Association, Atlanta, GA, April 1993, 25.
12. *Ibid.*, 8–9.

Notes to Chapter III   107

13. John O'Leary, "Fewer Parents Find Place for Children in First-Choice School," *London Times*, 31 December 1993.
14. *Ibid.*
15. Association of Metropolitan Authorities, *Choice of School: A Survey, 1992–1993* (London: Association of Metropolitan Authorities, 1993), 6–9.
16. *Ibid.*, 13–14.
17. Stephen J. Ball, Richard Bowe, and Sharon Gewirtz, Project Paper No. 3, Markets in Secondary Education Project, King's College, University of London, 1992.
18. Ron Glatter and Philip Woods, "The Impact of Competition and Choice on Parents and Schools," conference paper, University of Bristol, March 1993.
19. Barry Bastow, 193.
20. Ron Glatter and Philip Woods, 61.
21. Among the studies pointing to this conclusion are those from Scotland, where open enrollment has existed since 1982. See Frank Echols, Andrew McPherson, and J. Douglas Willms, "Parental Choice in Scotland," *Journal of Education Policy* 5, no. 3, 1990, 207–22.
22. Neville Beischer, "A Month-by-Month Admissions Plan," *Times Educational Supplement*, 3 June 1994.
23. The research from the Parental and School Choice Interaction Study, Centre for Educational Policy and Management, The Open University, leads to this conclusion.
24. Some of these examples are drawn from the research papers of Stephen Ball at King's College, University of London.
25. Philip Woods, 8.
26. Michael Adler, "An Alternative Approach to Parental Choice," National Commission on Education, Briefing Paper No. 13, March 1993; and Geoffrey Walford, "Selection for Secondary Schooling," National Commission on Education, Briefing Paper No. 7, October 1992.
27. Ernie Cave and Cyril Wilkinson, eds., *Local Management of Schools* (London: Routledge, 1990), 3.
28. Nick Holdsworth, "When Bigger Is Not Better," *Times Educational Supplement*, 1 July 1994.
29. Michael Adler, "An Alternative Approach to Parental Choice."

30. Organization for Economic Cooperation and Development, *School: A Matter of Choice* (Paris: OECD, 1993), 65.

CHAPTER IV   *The Picture of Reform*

1. "State Education—What Parents Want," a report by the MORI polling organization for *Reader's Digest*, June–July 1994.
2. George F. Madaus and Thomas Kellaghan, "The British Experience with Authentic Testing," *Phi Delta Kappan*, February 1993, 468.
3. Vivian Williams, ed., *Towards Self-Managing Schools* (London: Cassell, 1995), 20.

INDEX

INDEX

accountability, 91–92
Adler, Michael, 84–85
ADT College, 61
A-levels, 23, 61
Anderson, Keith (Gloucestershire), 43, 47, 76
Andrews, Clive (City Technology College Trust), 64
appeals of parental choice decisions, 78
assessment of students, 13, 25–31, 89–90
Association of Metropolitan Authorities, 44, 77–78
attainment targets, 13
autonomy, xiv, 33–67, 91

Bacon's CTC (London), 63
Baker, Kenneth, 12, 16, 71
Ball, Stephen, 41–42
Barber, Michael, 12
Beattie, Brigid (Burntwood School), 17, 22, 52–53, 72, 73, 78, 81
behavioral problem students, 54
Beischer, Neville, 80
bilingual education, 37
Black, Paul, 26, 29
boycott of standardized tests, 17, 30
Boyer, Ernest L., v, ix, xi–xviii, 66
Brighouse, Tim (Birmingham), 43–44, 47, 80, 92

British Record Industry Trust, 61, 65
Brooke, K. H. (Garth Hill School), 17, 36, 81
Brooke Weston school, 60–61
Burntwood School (London), 5–6, 17, 51, 52, 71–75, 77
Business and Technology Education Council, 23
Butler Act of 1944, 70

Callaghan, James, 10–11
Cambridgeshire, 36
Camden LEA, 43
Cassells, Sir John, 85
Centre for Educational Studies, 41–42
Centre for Policy Studies, 16
certificates, 61–62
charter schools, 33–34, 67, 91. *See also* Grant-maintained schools
checklists as assessment tool, 29
Cherwell School (Oxford), 22, 41, 45, 83, 84
Chicago schools, 34
Chubb, John E., 57, 91
City Technology College Trust, 64
city technology colleges, 5, 59–65
Clarke, Bernard (Peers School), 83
class differences in school choice, 78–79
Coleman, Marianne, 54

competition for places, 77–78
competition for students, 6, 79–82
comprehensive schools, 71
conservation of resources, 40
Conservative Party, 35, 47, 49, 69–70, 93
Coopers and Lybrand Deloitte, 37
core subjects, 13
corporate sponsorship, 64–65
county schools, 76
criteria for school choice, 75
cross-curricular themes, 22
cultural values and school choice, 78
curriculum, national, 3–4, 10–24, 89
curriculum and assessment, xv–xvi

Dearing, Sir Ron, 18, 22
declining enrollment, 82–83
democratic institutions, 91–92
Department for Education (U.K.), 53, 56
Derbyshire, 47
devolution of control, 65–66
disadvantaged students, xiii
Dixons CTC, 61
Djanogly school (Nottingham), 61
Downes, Peter (Hinchingbrooke School), 77, 81, 84

Eastbourne schools, 37, 39–40
economy needed skilled workers, 11–12
Education Act of 1944, 10
Education Act of 1993, 53
Education Reform Act of 1988, xi, xv, 25–26, 35, 48, 49, 93
equal access, 91
exclusions and expulsions by GM schools, 54

financing, 20, 90–91
  of CTCs, 64
  and governors, 47
  and grant-maintained schools, 51–52, 54–55
  under LMS, 36–41
France, 12, 16
Friedag, Torsten, 62
Funding Agency for Schools, 56

Garth Hill School (Berkshire), 45–46, 81
general schools budget, 37
Geoffrey Chaucer School (London), 83
Germany, 12
Gipps, Caroline, 28
Glatter, Ron, 74
Gloucestershire, 43, 76
GM. *See* Grant-maintained schools
Goals 2000 legislation, 9–10
governors, 44–46
grammar schools, 53, 71
grant-maintained schools, 5, 48–59, 64–65, 91
Grant-Maintained Schools Centre, 54
Greenwich schools, 40
group moderation, 27

Hackney schools, 46–47
headteachers, 35, 41–42
Hertfordshire, 54
Hinchingbrooke School (Cambridgeshire), 40, 77, 82
Horner, Marcus, 62
Howlett, Elizabeth, 44, 73

independent examinations boards, 7
inspection, xvi

Institute for Education (University of London), 46

Jackson, Howard, 73, 77
Japan, 12
Jenkins, Peter (Bacon's College), 63–64
Joseph, Keith, 16

Kent schools, 53, 54, 55–56
Kentucky, 34
Kingshurst school, 62
Knight, Cecil (Small Heath School), 51

Labor Party, 35, 58
Lawton, Denis, 24
LEAs. See Local education authorities
Leicestershire, 20
LMS. See Local management of schools (LMS)
local control, 4–5, 7
local education authorities, xiv–xv
 and Labor Party, 35
 and LMS, 42–44
local management of schools (LMS), 34–48, 58–59, 64–65, 90–91
Local Schools Information, 58
London Docklands Development Corporation, 63

Maclure, Stuart, 48
marketing of schools, 80–82, 92
materials expenditures under local management, 39
mathematics, 9
Mitchell, Peter (Camden Council), 43, 44
Moe, Terry M., 57, 91
morale, 41, 64
multiple-choice testing, 26, 90

Naismith, Donald (Wandsworth Council), 73
National Center on Education and the Economy, 30–31
National Council of Teachers of Mathematics, 89
National Curriculum Council, 17, 19
national government, xii, 14, 18
National Union of Teachers, 12
New Standards Project, 30–31
Northumberland, 76

Office of Standards in Education, 42
open enrollment, 6, 70
opting out, 7, 49–52, 58
Organization for Economic Cooperation and Development, 85
oversight, xiii

parent governors, 45
Parental and School Choice Interaction Study (PASCI), 74, 79
parents, xv, 47, 88
 and GM schools, 57
 and school choice, 69, 92
PASCI. See Parental and School Choice Interaction Study (PASCI)
Peers School (Oxfordshire), 83
per-capita funding, 6, 36–38, 66, 82, 92–93
Performing Arts and Technology School, 60, 61, 65
peripatetic teachers, 43
Perkins, Kizzy, 62
politicians, 87
portfolio assessment, 26, 90

power sharing among governmental units, 56, 87
primary schools, 21
principals. *See* Headteachers
Pryke, Roy (Kent), 54, 56

recruitment of students, 5–6, 71–72, 80
regional coordination, 87
religious education, 8, 10, 13, 70
resource allocation formula, 38
Roberts, Martin (Cherwell School), 4, 22, 23, 41, 45, 84
Romeo and Juliet controversy, 46
Royal Society for the Encouragement of Arts, Manufactures and Commerce (RSA), 23
RSA. *See* Royal Society for the Encouragement of Arts, Manufactures and Commerce (RSA)

salaries, 38–39
SATs. *See* Standard assessment tasks (SATs)
school boards, 66. *See also* Governors
school choice, xii–xiii, xvi, 57, 69–85
School Curriculum and Assessment Authority, 7, 13–14, 17–18, 88, 89
school districts, xiii–xiv, xv, 66. *See also* Local education authorities
school performance tables, 29
school-based management in U.S., 34
science curriculum, 15
Scotland, 84
secondary schools, 22
selective schools, 73

CTCs, 62
GM schools, 53–54
Small Heath School (Birmingham), 4–5, 50–51
snobbishness in GM schools, 54–55
Sofer, Ann, 21
Southwark, 46
Southwark Diocesan Board of Education, 63
special education, 37
standard assessment tasks (SATs), 26–27
standards, xii, 3–4, 6–7, 9–31, 57–58, 88, 89
state intervention in school failures, xvii
subject advisory groups, 18–19
support staff, 40
Szemerenyi, Stephen (Finchley Catholic High School), 36

Task Group on Assessment and Testing (TGAT), 26
teacher training, 19–20, 28
teacher unions in the U.S., 66
teachers
    and assessment of students, 26, 27
    and CTCs, 60
    need for involvement, 24, 88
    objections to curriculum reform, 14–15, 17
Teachers' Pay and Conditions Act, 60
teaching methods, 22
testing, standardized, 25, 26–30, 75–76
TGAT. *See* Task Group on Assessment and Testing (TGAT)
Thatcher, Margaret, 16, 69

Thomas Telford school (Shropshire), 60
transportation problems and school choice, 76–77

University of Pittsburgh, 31
U.S. Department of Education, 88
U.S. implications
   autonomy, 65–67
   curriculum reform, 24–25
   testing, 29–30

vocational or technical schools, 71
Wandsworth schools, 44, 51, 72–73
whole-class teaching, 22
Woods, Philip, 75
Wright Robinson High School, 6, 80

Ministry of Education & Training
MET Library
13th Floor, Mowat Block, Queen's Park
Toronto   M7A 1L2